Early Stages

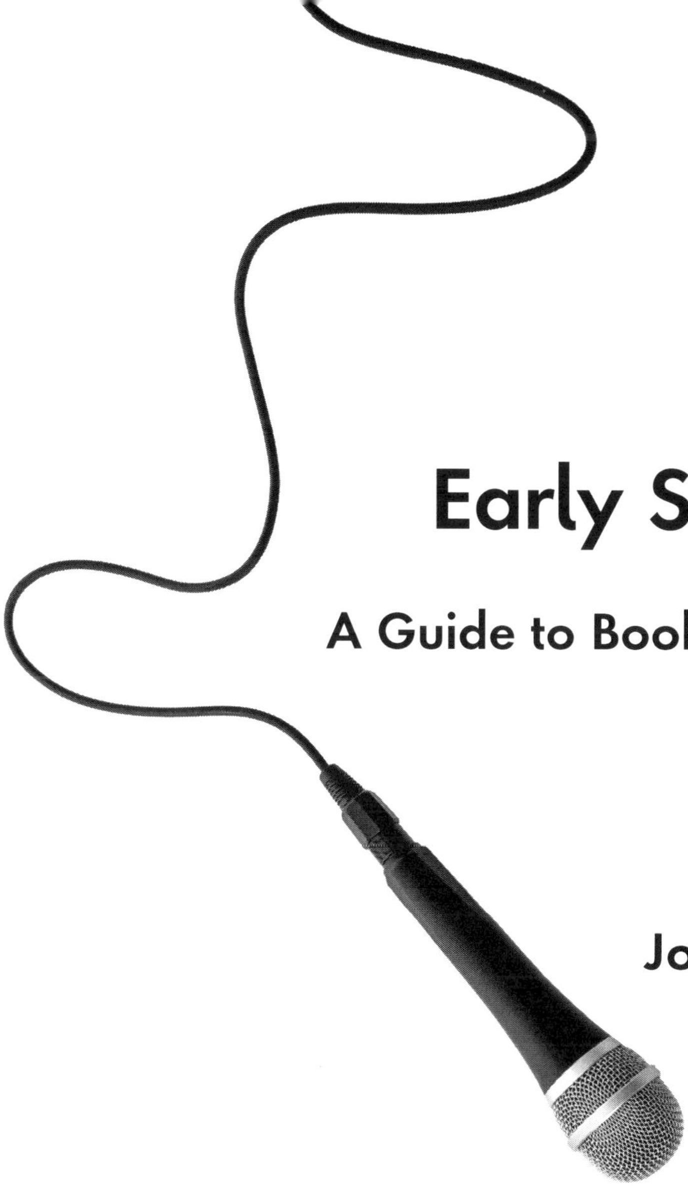

Early Stages

A Guide to Booking Gigs

Joe Ogden

First published 2019 by
Joe Ogden
joe@earlystagesbook.com

Text copyright © Joe Ogden 2019

ISBN 978-84-09-11774-1
EISBN 978-84-09-12401-5

Designed and typeset by Sandra Friesen

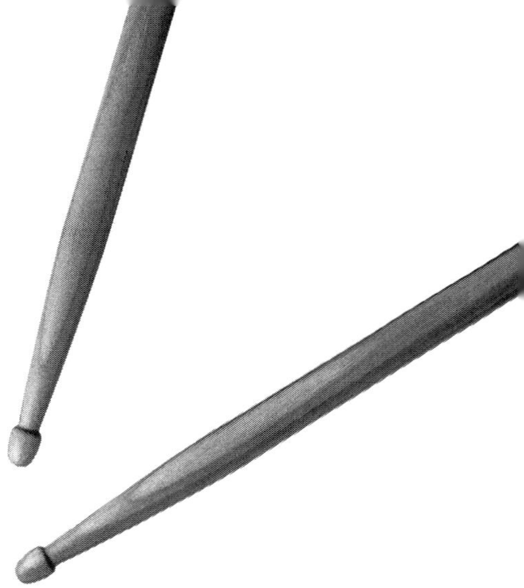

Contents

The Background

HR PERSON: After careful consideration, Mr Ogden, I'm pleased to say we'd like to offer you the job.

ME: Ah, brilliant. That's great news.

HR PERSON: We have one position in the offal room and one in the gut room. Which would you prefer?

ME: Hmm. Offal, please.

HR PERSON: OK, great. The shift in that room is 6 a.m. until 2.30 p.m. When can you start?

ME: Whenever you want me. I'm good to go.

The town I'm from is near Burnley, about thirty miles north of Manchester. Once, most people there would have worked in one of the many cotton mills in the area. A lot of my family were weavers, going back generations. Even my mum had been earlier in her life. However, when I was growing up almost all of the mills had either been demolished or had closed. By the time I was 18, all but one of us in my band had managed to get jobs at the local slaughterhouse and we started within a fortnight of each other. The guitarist was sent to pork and lamb, the singer to packing and I was in offal. I drew the short straw, but at least I didn't end up in the gut room.

Playing an instrument and being in a band allowed for some adventuring outside of my town. A way to go and explore and to earn some money doing what I loved to do, which was going to pubs ... I mean playing gigs. My fellow band members and I wanted to play as many gigs as we could, anywhere that would have us. And I was happy to book those gigs.

Speaking on the phone was daunting at first, especially when it was with proper grown-ups who didn't like music anymore, or musicians – or phone calls. But I didn't mind it. I got a kick out of it, especially breaking the news that we'd landed another show and we were getting paid for it.

We practised, played many gigs locally and soon enough we were travelling to far more glamorous parts of the world. I remember one run I booked which took us to Grimsby, Barnsley, Doncaster, Rotherham, Rochdale, Stockport, Blackburn and Wakefield.

You've got to start somewhere.

In 2005, I left home and moved to London to start a music performance degree at Drum Tech, which at the time was said to be one of the top contemporary music schools in Europe. I'd imagined being right in the thick of London life and the music scene there, but the reality was different. I actually played fewer gigs when I was in London than I had done back at home. About eighteen months after starting at Drum Tech, I got a call from a promoter who had given one of my old bands and I some guidance in the early days. He worked at a reputable music management firm in Manchester. One of the bands they were managing – The Jakpot – had lost their drummer. I say 'lost' – he wasn't dead; he'd got into a fight with a bouncer and had broken his wrist. So, they fired him and were holding auditions for a replacement.

The band had a run of UK shows and a European club tour confirmed, along with some solid press support, so I went for it and got the job. Eventually, commuting to the gigs from London every week became tedious, so I threw in the towel at Drum Tech and moved to Manchester to give it a real go. We had a whale of a time on the road in the UK and Europe; tour buses, sell-out shows, proper riders, free bars, hotels, fans, autographs, radio sessions. It was great, I loved it.

When I first joined the band, I was sent a list of the upcoming shows and a number of the German dates had 'Private Helicopter' written next to them. Obviously, I assumed (and told everyone) that we were going to be ferried around in a helicopter between venues. However, that is not what happened: Private Helicopter was just the name of the company promoting those shows. The mode of transport between them was a van. Firmly on the ground. In fact, it was so unglamorous that part of the deal between a promoter and one venue was that the promoter would clean the venue after the show. But he left before we did and following our packed headline show – and a final round of Jägermeister – we had to sweep the whole place before we were allowed out with our gear.

Rock'n'roll.

After the third jaunt to Europe, interest in the band had waned significantly in the UK. Music trends had moved on, as they will, and the band eventually split up in 2007.

In 2008, I joined that same management company in Manchester and began booking shows for other bands on the roster. I eventually began booking gigs for artists that weren't on the company's management roster and, by 2010, I had founded the booking agency arm of the business. I was running my own agency and I was getting paid for it.

Eighteen months later, in January 2012, I was offered a job at one of the major agencies in London. Their roster contained huge, internationally acclaimed artists. The musical icons of a generation. The stadium-fillers. The festival headliners. It was a fantastic opportunity. Over the course of almost five years, I scouted for new artists, built my own roster and booked many tours under the mentorship of one of the directors and senior agents.

I was set on working in music from the age of 7, when I started playing drums. I was excited to play in bands and waited impatiently for the best part of eight years, practising every day while all my mates were out playing kiss chase ... I mean football, on the back streets.

Here are some of the bands I was in – at least those I stayed in for a minimum of one gig:

Mainline 69	school band
Antimony	rock band
Kings of the Delmar	rockabilly punk band
Fantera	metal tribute band
The Jakpot	indie band
Superfly	wedding band
The Real Dolls	rock/hip-hop band
Emmott and the Butties	experimental band

(A butty is a sandwich, in case you didn't know. I was one of the Butties. True story.)

Success did not come when one of the bands I was in became 'big' – as you might have already guessed from that list. It came when I focused so much on booking shows that it ultimately led to me being an agent for a living. Here are the essential lessons I learned along the way. This is the book that I wish had existed when I was in bands.

The Content

I don't know who you are and I don't know what you want, but if it's money you're looking for, you might not have come to the right place.

What I can promise your band is a better chance. A chance of success. A chance to book more shows, to play better shows, to avoid risky shows and to eventually book your band all the way onto the radar of the right kinds of people.

If you can do all that, the money will come.

Here's what I am *not* going to tell you in this book:

Learn an instrument
Join a band
Write some songs
Rehearse the songs
Write some better songs
Record some songs
Play at open mic nights
Play at jam nights
Get good
Have the right attitude
Turn up on time
Network with other bands
Learn how to be nice to people
Learn how to share backline with other bands

Learn not to drink beer that belongs to other bands

Here's what I am also *not* going to cover in this book:

Artist management
Music production
Publishing deals
Record deals
Distribution deals
Music law
Contract law
Radio and TV
PR and marketing
International tour management
International immigration laws
Visas

Here's what I *am* going to talk about in this book:

How to get your band playing shows once *you* have covered the basics (the first of the two lists above) but before you have an agent and a professional team on board to advise, navigate through and take care of all the other areas (dealt with in the second list). I am going to focus on what I have many years of experience doing – getting gigs for bands. Not just for bands, though. You might be a singer-songwriter, a rapper, a DJ, a solo pianist or whatever. By band I mean your musical outfit, your group, your ensemble, your collective, yourself. You catch my drift. If you want to play live, you have come to the right place.

You're going to have to put in some work as well, though. This isn't a directory of promoter or venue contacts. This isn't a shortcut. This book provides my personal thoughts and suggestions along with hypothetical examples, to give you and your band something to work with. Think of it like an aid. A helping hand. This has its basis in the time I spent playing in bands and later as an agent. My experiences have been unique to me and therefore my approach to representing artists is also my own, inspired by the many words of wisdom and the advice I received from people with much more knowledge than I had.

You will finish this book with a clearer idea of how to think more like an agent, how to become more self-sufficient and, as a result, you'll be able to better position your band as a serious outfit for your fans, the music industry and the media. That doesn't necessarily mean you'll have loads more gigs and your band will get much more money. Not yet. It's about giving your band the best chance of success: the shows your band do not play can matter almost as much as the ones that they do play, regardless of the money on offer.

When it comes to booking shows, anyone can learn the fundamentals and apply themselves if they want to be more effective. It's about effort, it's about attitude, it's about determination, it's about persistence and it's about practise.

The Team

The best route to getting gigs is through an agent. There, I've said it.

The End.

(Please keep reading.)

Let's not skip past that. This is not a 'how to bypass the music industry' book. What good would that do? An agent, a manager, a publisher, a record label, a publicist, a radio plugger and a lawyer typically add up to equal *your team*, and your team can be vital in your band achieving success.

No household name artist has ever got to where they are by representing themselves all the way to the top. Although many will have done it in the early days when they were getting off the ground, if your band is aiming high, you will not be able to represent yourselves forever. You wouldn't want to either; you'll have enough to do. Additionally, no book in the world can be a substitute for what a real-life human agent or wider team can offer you, as long as they're good.

You're going to want an agent if you can get one. And a good agent will naturally want to devise a plan. A strategy. Shows will need to coincide with and support other activity, such as record releases and media coverage. Exclusivity around important shows also becomes crucial to building some demand, and the right agent will guide you on which shows to pursue and those to turn down.

How to build that team? First, find a good manager if you can, before an agent, publisher, label or anyone, really. The manager usually builds the team and makes sure everyone is working in sync. For example, they ensure the label have committed to a release date, the publicist and plugger have a defined timeline for building hype and the agent is booking a run of dates to correspond with the release. They oversee everything. Much of the music industry will not want to be involved with you until a good manager is on board. Equally, a bad manager can put people off working with your band, so be careful. You're going to develop a close working relationship with your manager and you need to agree on the direction for your band, so make sure you carefully consider that appointment.

Until you involve the professionals, you will have to be your own team. Maybe someone does the lion's share of the driving? Maybe someone is good at building websites? Maybe one of you has a garage to rehearse in? Or if you're a solo outfit, you probably do it all. But who's going to book all of the gigs? You need gigs to play to refine your live show and gain fans and exposure. You need gigs to invite potential managers and agents. Who's going to be your agent before you find a proper agent?

The music industry picks and chooses the artists it wants to work with – those that appear to have the potential of becoming successful, in turn making the industry professionals successful, including agents. Some artists play live for years before they get any serious industry attention. Let's also not ignore the fact that many artists never get any serious interest from managers or agents or never find the right people to represent them or in fact do not want representation.

Yet they still need gigs.

It can be detrimental to your band to get an agent *too* early. You may find you have less freedom to play at your mate's rooftop party for a crate of beer and a few sausage rolls; the kind of show that makes little impact on your profile but gives you an opportunity to hone your performance skills and develop a fan base before you play the more important shows.

Whatever your situation, if you do not have an agent then you need to be your own, and here's what you need to know:

- → The responsibilities of a promoter and how you can get them on board.
- → How to put together a stronger live schedule for your band.
- → How to enhance your band's brand and perceived success by playing the right shows.
- → What your band should be cautious of and when to be prepared to say 'No'.
- → The responsibilities of agents, how you can imitate them and how one could help you.
- → How you can better position your band to attract industry interest.

Here's how to become your own agent, until you can get a proper one.

The Launch

I'm aware that not everyone reading this book is in a brand-new band. Some will be only just ready to get stuck into doing some shows and others will be further along the path towards that arena tour. You're probably thinking, *Hang on, we 'launched' ages ago! What's this moron talking about?* Just hear me out, please.

Take this section as an opportunity to reflect on how you position yourselves, not just to promoters but to your fans. To the world.

I've worked with bands who have launched just with one song online, on a web page featuring the band's logo and a music link. That's it. No pictures. No gig history. Maybe not even contact details. Certainly no, *It all started when Pete met Fred in a kebab shop*.

Just one or two good songs with some mystery surrounding them and a list of some decent upcoming shows (if you have any yet) can often generate more interest than having too much content. Leave people wondering. *Is it a four-piece? Is that a synth? How do they recreate that weird didgeridoo sound live?* Get people talking and sharing.

There will be exceptions, with any famous family connections or if, for example, the singer has had some prior success in a different field. Modelling or acting, maybe. Perhaps some of your members were in a different band previously that received some level of attention. If the story is credible and it helps generate some early interest, then consider mentioning it, although I'd be careful how long you ride that wave for. You need to build your profile based on the band's own merits.

Even if you've been around the block a little and therefore aren't 'launching' as such, you can still apply some of these same principles to your online presence or to your approach to promoters. You don't need an extensive backstory emphasizing how long you've been around for and how many great (and terrible) shows you've played – that often just puts people off. It's like saying, 'Oh, hi there, look how long we've been around for, yet we still haven't really got anywhere.' You need to appear exciting and relevant *today*. If your band are not an established name outside of your local area, if you haven't 'made it' so to speak and any sniff of success you've had appears to be in the past, then you'll be lucky if people buy into your band's future. And that's across the board in the music industry, not just in the context of trying to get gigs. It includes any attempt you may make to get an agent interested.

Things need to appear to be happening for the band right *now*. If there's not much happening, make something happen. 'Launch' something. Announce something, using any medium in which your band communicates to the world. Here are some ideas for what you could announce, subject to what stage you're at:

A debut single
A headline show
A sell-out show
A new single
A new EP
A new music video
A residency
A collaboration

I'm sure you can think of some others.

Create a story. Get some attention. Bolster your position and you'll give promoters a reason to book your band. Depending on how well things are going for you, if you feel as if your fan base is diminishing and the interest in your band is decreasing then you might want to think about a name change and a relaunch. A fresh start could open new doors.

Is your music up to scratch? There are no excuses nowadays for poor recordings. Do some hustling, ask around, use some recording/sequencing software like GarageBand or Pro Tools, borrow some good studio mics. Whatever you need to do. Just make it sound good; it's down to you.

The launch pad:

- → Don't give too much information away when you're a relatively new outfit, retain some mystery.
- → Reference previous successes and notable connections only if they are credible.
- → Regardless of how established your band are locally, a long backstory does not necessarily help you.
- → Keep your band relevant and create interest in what you are doing now, or in the near future.
- → Make your recordings sound tip-top.

The Approach

The days of using snail mail to post your demo tape/CD/press pack/limited edition vinyl are over. Electronic Press Kits (EPKs) can do one, too. It's overload. It's too much information. To start off with, anyway.

Think of your approach to a promoter, or to an agent or a manager for that matter, as akin to meeting someone for the first time, in the pub. How much do you tell them about yourself? Probably the highlights, I'd imagine. A brief overview, maybe. You wouldn't give them a biography of yourself in a jiffy bag, would you? I hope not. Refrain from using social media or website contact/submission forms to put forward your band to promoters, too.

Imagine you're a promoter, working in-house at a venue. Who would introduce their band via the venue's social media page or the online submission form? Answer: someone that the promoter doesn't know and someone who is not an agent, because an agent would rarely, if ever, pitch an artist like that.

Using that approach doesn't mean your band are not good but it does show that you do not have representation. And that puts your band in a bucket. In a category. You're an unrepresented band, which could mean you're absolutely rubbish or that you're just getting off the ground and will become the next stadium headliner. Or anything in-between. But either way, you're in that same bucket as the others until there is a team on board. So, you need to stand out.

Imagine that same in-house promoter again. Who would put in the time to find out the promoter's name, before calling the venue to speak with them or to ask for their email address? An agent would – which means so should you.

I never booked any shows via social media. If I received an enquiry from a promoter via social media, I asked for their email address or phone number in order to follow up. I'd also question how seriously I should take any promoter who took the social media approach to me. As with everything, there will always be exceptions, but as a rule, when pitching your band to promoters, keep it professional and within established boundaries and you'll get better results. That's my experience.

Treat your first email or call to a promoter as an opportunity to plant a seed. To start a conversation. They're initially going to want some key information, maybe an idea of your social media following and a music link to click on. If you've played some noteworthy shows recently – like good festivals, support slots or sold-out headline shows – mention them. Share links to new music and, if you've had some good press, share that as well. One or two good and *recent* reviews will help your cause, but if you've been on the scene for a while, I'd hold back on sharing the three-and-a-half-star review published two years ago. Maybe you think it shows longevity and experience, but it doesn't really help.

Once you've sent that email, a follow-up call can be extremely effective. It's a chance to put them on the spot to try and get a commitment, if you approach it in the right way. Just don't be *too* pushy. Calls can also be the most effective initial form of communication, when it comes to your more old-school promoters such as pub landlords, concert secretaries at working men's clubs or basically anyone who started promoting in the 1970s or earlier. Just work out the best approach for the kind of person you're targeting. As you build relationships with promoters, you'll learn how best to communicate with them individually, and how to get an answer. If you don't know much about the person you are contacting, I would try the email approach first and see how you get on. You also have a 'reason for the call' if you have emailed first, as opposed to making a cold call.

Recommendations and referrals go a long way in any industry. If you can get an introduction to a promoter through someone you know, or at least be able to mention a mutual connection who means something, you're going to give yourself a better chance of hearing back. Mentioning well-known and respected promoters who have booked your band is a good example of this approach. If you say the right name to some promoters, they realize they're dealing with a serious outfit who are worth paying attention to. Equally, if you've been playing sketchy shows or working with promoters with a bad reputation, you'll be associated with them and good promoters may keep their distance.

When speaking with a promoter, be clear about a window of availability that ties in with some activity, e.g. other shows (not in the same town), a release or some press, or whatever. Just something. Create a timeframe that provides a compelling reason for the promoter to get on board sooner rather than later. I.e. if they don't commit to booking your band now, they will be left out of the upcoming run of shows involving other, cooler, younger, better-looking and more cutting-edge promoters. If you're too vague about availability or the type of show you're looking for, you might struggle to prompt that promoter to make an offer, so try to narrow it down a bit.

On the approach:

- → Keep your approach concise and don't overload a new contact with excessive amounts of information.
- → When booking a gig, don't forget that you're approaching a promoter (i.e. a person), not a venue (i.e. a building). Do your research and know who you're contacting and how best to reach them.
- → Tell promoters which other reputable industry figures – locally or nationally – have been supportive of your band.
- → Create some urgency by being specific about what you want within a timeframe that ties in with other planned activity.

The Contacts

It's not just who you know, it's what you know. And what I know is that when I started out, I didn't know any promoters whatsoever. None. Nor did I have any family connections to any promoters or access to a contacts list. I was starting from scratch, as you have also probably had to do.

I didn't know that I wanted to become an agent, though. I was just in a band that needed some gigs. Like you. Needs must. As I established myself as a gig booker and as I became more active, the more contacts I made.

I started with a phone and a copy of the Yellow Pages, and built up enough of a contact base to start my own agency. My brother was the guitarist in my band back in those early days and we teamed up. While I called landlords and promoters and made a nuisance of myself, he kept researching online and compiling contact names and numbers for other bookers and venues. We also researched where the bands that we liked, or had played with, were playing and shortlisted those venues and promoters. We were literally doing this at the same time, me in one room and him in the other. Once I'd exhausted my list and sufficiently embarrassed myself on the phone, he'd walk in with another list and I'd start all over again. Before we knew it, we had a solid run of shows booked. I remember people asking us how we'd got so many shows and all we'd done is some basic research, started building a list and picked up the phone.

That's it.

The more shows I booked, the more shows we played, and the more shows we played, the more the promoters got in contact with us. The more bands we played with, the more introductions we could get to other promoters and potential support slots became available with those other bands.

And so ... the spreadsheet grew.

Remember, a promoter is for life, not just for Christmas. Let me rephrase that. If you become connected with a good promoter, you're not going to play only one show with them. Not always, anyway. It depends what kind of promoter they are, but the research you've put in and your approach to that promoter will not necessarily just be for one show. If they're good and become *your* promoter in that respective town or city, you're potentially going to play many shows with them. Keep that in mind when you do a first show with a promoter. It's like you're both dipping your toe in the water. Establishing relationships with good promoters is essential.

If you're struggling to find who to contact to try and book a gig at a specific venue, make sure that submitting a form on a website is your last resort. You need to be smarter than that. You need to interact directly with a human whose name you know. Yeah, yeah, I know humans read the submission forms. But I mean proper interaction. Old-school interaction. A conversation. A back and forth. Questions and answers. That's when you can start to try and persuade someone.

Which bands do you know who have played at that venue before? Ask them for details of the promoter. If you make an impression with promoters, they'll tell other promoters about you, too. They might also introduce you to them if they're not in competition.

When it comes to many festivals and events, you're also going to be lucky to find the booker's contact details on the website and it's obvious why. They'd be inundated by bands, which is the last thing they want. Hence the online submission form or a generic email address. It's just to keep people at bay. Most festival promoters will have a list of artists they want to approach (via the agent) to play at their event. Your band will probably not be on that list, which means they're not going to be contacting you. So, you need to contact the promoter:

Is there a main promoter behind the event, or is it independent?
Have you played any shows with them before?
Which bookers are responsible for which stages?
How can you reach them?
Who else is playing?
Who can make an introduction?

Look on social media. See if there have been any articles in the news about the event. Find a name for a booker. If there's an office number, call it. If you get fobbed off with some generic email address, try and guess what the booker's email address is based on their name and the company's web URL.

I know I said at the beginning that I wouldn't tell you to network with other bands, but you need to network with other bands. Network with promoters. Network with anyone you can. Make yourself known and be nice. Follow up with them after the show.

Keep in touch and add them to the spreadsheet – it's not going to build itself.

Let me build a summary:

→ Avoid online artist submission forms and make initial contact with anyone in a personal manner wherever possible.

- → Learn what to look for online to help work out who's behind an event and how you can contact them directly.
- → Try to establish and build relationships with good promoters – they can be integral early champions for your band and are sometimes gateways to the wider music industry.
- → Do not buy someone a promoter for Christmas.

The Process

There is a standard process that goes on between agents and promoters when it comes to booking artists to play shows.

When I was playing in bands, it would have been hugely beneficial for me to understand how it all works on the industry side. Specifically, to know how a good show or a tour gets booked. Was it all favours between industry bigwigs? Loads of back-scratching and ego-stroking? Was it a who-you-know-not-what-you-know type of affair? There is some of that going on for sure, but a lot of successful agents also get good results by being proactive. A step ahead. Not only by submitting their artists for anything and everything that is suitable and keeping them on the radar of good promoters, but by finding the promising artists to represent in the first place. The right attitude with the right connections is the ideal combination and that goes for everyone.

Generally, promoters are responsible for organizing shows/gigs/concerts/live performances – call them what you will – and the integral element of the event is the artist on the bill. There are some exceptions to this and key differences between certain kinds of promoters, but we'll come on to them later. To begin with, in simple terms, if an artist has an agent, then any promoter interested in the artist will contact the agent to ask about booking them to play a show. Or, the agent will contact a promoter they think might be interested in booking the artist to play a show.

Based on that conversation, the promoter may want to make an offer to the artist. The agent will then speak to the manager about it. The manager is the boss of all members of the band's team. When it comes to accepting or declining offers, the manager is responsible for making the decision and may consult with the artist and other members of the team, such as the label. But ultimately, it's the manager who makes the call and informs the agent of the decision. Based on that decision, the agent will either tell the promoter that they are interested or are not.

When an agent makes the initial approach and contacts a promoter, the strength of their pitch and the status of that agent within the industry plays a big part in how that promoter responds. The relationship between the respective agent and promoter also matters, of course.

The process of an agent booking a show for an up-and-coming artist could go something like the list below. In this example, let's say the band are new, the agent has just added them to their roster and the agent is relatively new to the industry as well:

- → Agent contacts promoter with pitch about an artist.
- → Promoter looks at/listens to what has been sent, considers response before not responding.
- → Agent waits a couple of days before calling promoter to make sure email was received.
- → Promoter says they haven't seen the email and asks for it to be re-sent.
- → Agent re-sends email.
- → Promoter responds two days later expressing interest (to varying degrees) and asks what fee the agent is looking for.
- → Agent responds using chosen initial negotiation technique.
- → Promoter responds with terrible offer.

And so begins the back and forth before a provisional deal is reached. The agent will either send the offer straight to the artist's manager or, if the show would form part of a tour, they will collect multiple offers together before presenting a schedule of shows to the manager including everything.

The manager will look at the numbers and then call the agent to give them a hard time … I mean, discuss the offers. If all is well and the decision is in the affirmative, they will ask the agent to confirm the show.

The agent will then contact the promoter to confirm the show.

GIG BOOKED!

OK, we're back in the room. That is *one* way it can go and is one very specific example. The promoter might also never have responded or might have come back immediately. The agent might have been a major player in the business and the promoter is over the moon about being approached. The promoter might have been a major player in the business and cannot believe the agent thought they'd be interested. The band could have been terrible and no promoter could believe the agent thought they'd be interested.

That example is also based on there being a manager and agent on board. Your band probably has neither and you're acting as both, which is what many, if not all, artists experience at one time. Therefore, understanding what promoters are familiar with when it comes to the gig-booking process will help you a lot because, of course, they are always involved when it comes to booking your band to play shows.

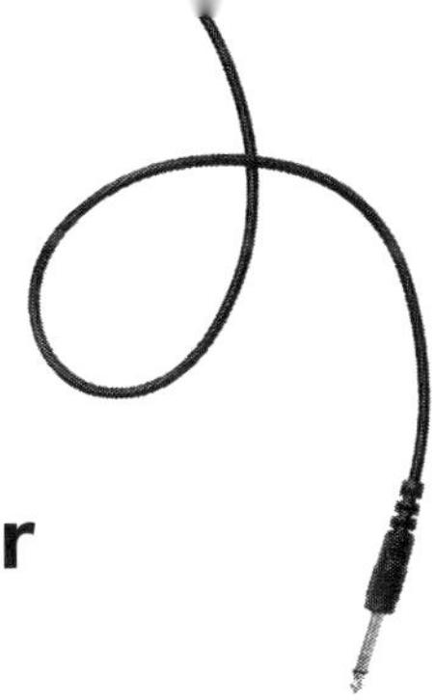

The Promoter

When it comes to your usual headline show in a venue, the person who hires the venue for the band to play the show is a promoter. It's not an agent or a manager, or a label. It's an in-house promoter or an external promoter. 'Promoter' is a catch-all term. It can refer to many different types of roles that involve booking bands to play shows.

The classic concert promoter sees the potential in an artist and is willing to foot the costs up front to arrange a performance by the artist. The promoter hires the venue of choice and they are also responsible for promoting (i.e. marketing) the show to enough people to encourage a healthy attendance, a figure which in most cases is measured in ticket sales. The promoter is the mediator between the artist and the venue, and the show would not happen without a promoter of some form. They take the financial risk and negotiate the deal with the artist (or their agent) for the artist to perform. If a fair deal is agreed, the promoter will go on to cover their costs and make a profit from the show from ticket sales.

What's in it for the promoter? Money. Oh, and enjoyment. However, both of those depend largely on how successful they are. They might also want to grow their business and establish themselves, and the artists and agents they work with will have a big impact on that.

A good promoter will get the message out there about your band's show. They will know the local music scene and will use effective marketing methods to connect with the right audience:

- Flyer distribution
- Poster placement
- Mail-outs
- Social media ads
- Local press listings
- Print ads
- Student promotions
- Billboards
- Local radio ads

'Promoter' can also describe someone who is employed by a venue or a festival to take care of a specific event. This is someone who is responsible for putting together some or all of a line-up and may, or may not, be involved literally in *promoting* (i.e. marketing) the show. They may sometimes be more of a 'curator' than a 'promoter'. It's not an easily defined role but it's essential to understand the different kinds of promoters and the context of how they operate before you approach them.

Let's look at some of the main promoter categories.

Local promoters are often independent businesses and are specific to a city or area. They usually book across a range of venues of different shapes and sizes. Local promoters can be great champions for your band and great to get on board early. You should find those in your nearest cities to start off with and gradually, as your national profile grows, go on to find the good ones in all cities in which you want your band to play.

If you get an enthusiastic local promoter on side, you'll be in a strong position to get some good shows, e.g. at good club nights with an established audience and as the 'local opener' for touring artists playing in the city. Most local promoters will expect a level of loyalty from you when your profile grows, i.e., when an artist has established enough fans to play their own headline show, the promoter would like to get first refusal on promoting that headline show in return for having helped the artist on their way to getting those fans. It's common sense, really.

Local promoters can often find themselves competing with national promoters at the point at which national promoters take an interest in an artist that the local promoter has been helping and nurturing. Think of it like this – there is no real money in it for any promoter until the artist gets some serious traction and is worth a large number of tickets in that city. That's when there is some potential profit from shows (see The Deal section) and if at that point the band choose to go with a national promoter in that city, it can be a real blow for the local one, as you would imagine.

One strong advantage a local promoter has over national promoters is that they're on the ground in that city. They're based there. They really understand the place and the audience; the range of suitable venues and capacities; the good and bad nights of the week; the key local festivities/events and the dates to avoid in case of any clashes; the areas, venues and nights that are popular with students; and the price that gig-goers in that city are comfortable paying for a ticket. All the intel you want from a promoter when you're working with them, whichever city they may be in. They may also run or be involved in good new music festivals and other local events that could really help your band get some exposure.

A limitation a local promoter may have is their ability to scale up to the big venues, as and when the artist gets to that point. It depends on the size of the promoter and how much financial risk they're able and willing to take, but long before you're facing that scenario, you're going to have an agent on board to take care of things anyway.

National promoters are organizations that promote in venues across all cities. Technically they promote *anywhere* but tend to concentrate mostly on the 'main' cities before expanding, depending on the artist's profile and the demand for shows. By 'main' cities I mean those with the bigger populations.

National promoters are the heavyweights and their marketing is at a national level, meaning their reach is significant. Nowadays, they are involved in most tours you see on sale. They sometimes get on board early with new artists and can help hugely because they promote most of the biggest shows in the country and have influence with some of the big managers, agents and artists. Some amazing support slots could come via these promoters and they are often involved in festivals, too. The right promoter could give your band a leg-up to play on some great line-ups that could have a big impact.

Historically, national promoters would dip their toe in the water with a new artist by co-promoting shows with local promoters or with club/venue promoters. It's a way of putting their name to the show while the artist is in the ascendant and it *can* be a worthwhile association for the artist as it can look like a step up, i.e. a big-name promoter that most music fans across the country have heard of is now involved. It can also be perceived within the music industry as good progress.

In the past, national promoters waited until an agent began sniffing around before getting too involved with a new artist. The risk for them otherwise, if an agent started to represent the artist and the promoter didn't have a relationship with the agent, was that the agent could always just offer the artist to a different promoter based on their own preferences or those of the manager. Many experienced promoters still hold back somewhat until it becomes obvious who is going to be representing the band at a manager or agent level. But some national promoters go the other way and try and get on board with the artist before an agent gets involved. That can sometimes be a good thing for the artist and the incoming agent, depending on who the promoter is, or it can end up in a tricky situation if the agent doesn't believe that the promoter is right for the artist, despite how involved they have been up to that point.

It can get quite political when it comes to deciding which national promoters should be involved with an artist and in particular which promoter is granted London as one of their cities. Your best bet is to take all the help you can get from national promoters but be conscious that it won't be long before an agent comes on board, so let them decide the best steps forward from there. In fact, you can use that interest from a big promoter as a reason to approach or re-approach any agents you're trying to get on board.

Promotion becomes a little more straightforward in some respects when the artist is more established. With bigger shows comes increased marketing budgets and therefore the promotional techniques become more typical and mainstream, e.g. press ads, radio ads and billboards. But a national promoter can be at a disadvantage when it comes to the on-the-ground understanding and marketing techniques that a local promoter often excels at, especially with smaller shows. Here, marketing often needs to be more inventive as budgets are tighter and it may not be as clear-cut to understand how to reach the fans, as the artist is relatively new. Local tastemaker blog support can help, as can social media campaigns and effective poster/flyer placement around town. These can make a big difference for those smaller-capacity shows. It's not to say that national promoters can't do all aspects of promotion and marketing, just that local promoters can understand their city that bit more.

A word of warning: be careful what you commit to with the multinational/corporate promoters and, whatever you do, don't sign any contracts or accept any 'loans' that commit your band to working exclusively with them. Think of it as like being arrested and interrogated by the police – you need professional representation at that point.

In-house promoters are employed by a venue and are responsible for its events programme throughout the year. Apart from when the venue is hired out, for example, by local promoters and national promoters. The same benefits are shared with venue promoters and good local promoters. They are able to offer good support slots and club night shows when you're getting off the ground.

When you get to the stage where you're headlining shows and selling tickets, some of the best deals can be done directly with venues as opposed to involving an external promoter. In-house promoters will often have the best rental and production rates available to them, as they're essentially hiring the venue from themselves. The venue's marketing team should also understand the local market and how to effectively promote the shows to the right audience in order to fill their venue.

A drawback with in-house promoters is that, depending on how flexible their arrangement with the respective venue is, they may be limited to only promoting shows in that venue. However, some in-house promoters can and will promote in rival venues, too, so it is always worth checking. If not, though, when you're at the point that your band want to play in a different venue in that city, you're either going to need to work with a local or national promoter or with the alternative venue's in-house promoter directly.

Festivals often have one primary booker or booking team responsible for curating the main stage line-ups, with other bookers sometimes responsible for smaller stages and fringe events. Together, they create the full festival line-up.

Established festivals sell a lot of tickets based on the headliners alone. Profile and size of the artists across the rest of the line-up remain important factors, though the booker might also be looking for interesting/exciting/ quirky live acts to keep the line-up varied.

Therefore, genre, live performance style and quality of the live show are also important factors for bookers when they're considering your band. If you're good live, it's always a good idea to invite festival bookers along to upcoming shows for them to get a better understanding of if, and where you might fit on the bill. You might get booked onto a festival line-up simply because you're good and interesting live, and not because you're worth tickets.

When approaching festival bookers to pitch your band, letting them know which other well-known and credible events have booked you already *can* help, if there aren't too many. If the band played some good festivals last year, then you could mention them as it can look like the band are at a certain level, but only as long as there is something happening for the band this year, too. You won't get booked solely off the back of a good summer last year.

If you have a packed summer schedule this year, don't risk putting off the promoter by shouting about *all* of the festivals the band are playing at, as offering your band a slot on their line-up won't feel as exclusive, which means they might not book you. Mention two or three and, if they're not too nearby or similar in line-up and the type of audience they attract, it might help you get some interest.

Pub landlords are mostly interested in booking bands who can also (or only) play covers. Gigs are most common on Friday and Saturday nights and tend to require the band to play two forty-five-minute sets. *'Do you play any AC/DC?'*

Traditional pubs very rarely charge on the door, so landlords rely on bar take alone to cover their costs. However, inner city-type pubs – those that are trendy, have a proper live room and sell tickets for gigs – should be thought of more like your regular music venues.

Fun-time Freda is that pal from earlier with the rooftop and the sausage rolls, and also represents every other friend and local party organizer who can offer your band a stage to play on.

Any promoter you come across may also be involved in promoting regular nights and, by that, I mean an event of a particular genre in a venue with an established crowd. It could be an indie club night. It could be a hip-hop night. It could be a folk night. It might be a combination of live acts and DJs. Promoters may use slots on the bill at a popular night to give an artist some exposure and to help them build a fan base.

Remember that a promoter's job is to take risks and, in most cases, they are tastemakers responsible for finding either bands that people want to see now or bands that people will want to see by the time the show comes around. They're probably not going to book your band to headline a ticketed show if you don't have many fans. However, even if the band aren't worth many tickets yet, the promoter might still want to offer a show if you're good live and there's a bit of a buzz. It could still be beneficial to certain promoters for your band to play on one of their support bills or club nights, to help develop their own reputation as a tastemaker or talent spotter. Or you never know, they might just want to help you out.

Good promoters are also in touch with agents very often because they book touring artists, so if your name keeps cropping up, for example as a local support suggestion for a bigger artist, then you're eventually going to be on the radar of agents. Probably. Some promoters will go out of their way to tip off agents if they have a good relationship with them and there's enough of a buzz about a band. So, make a good impression with the right kind of promoters and, if an agent is what you want, you're going to have a better chance of getting one.

The most important thing for promoters, though, is that they need to make money to continue doing what they do, which will mean mostly booking established artists to be in with a chance of making a profit from shows. Whether they're independent or are employed by a venue or promotions company, the financial bottom line is critical in determining how long they can continue promoting shows.

It's very competitive and is not an easy job.

What not to forget:

- → Clearly understanding the promoter's role and the different types of promoter that exist will help you to improve your approach.
- → Local promoters are crucial for your band – in the early days and beyond.
- → In-house promoters at venues are equally as important throughout your career in providing a stage and an audience.
- → National promoters can provide game-changing opportunities and often have significant influence with agents and managers.
- → Festival promoters hold the key to major opportunities for your band – we'll talk more about them later in the book.
- → Pub landlords like covers and big local followings.

The Email

When approaching promoters for the first time, keep it brief. Highlight some key points, include a link to one or two killer songs and any recent press coverage (if there is anything yet) and be specific about what you're getting in touch about. You might have their attention for one minute, or less. Make it count.

Your band are not going to get a gig *just* because you can write well and because you know the difference between 'there', 'their' and 'they're'. But if your email is well-written and concise, it will look professional and that means the recipient will *probably* read it, which is a good start.

Do you know what else will help make them read the email? An email addressed to them personally which is obviously not generic. Make it personalized. The worst thing you can do when emailing promoters is to just send one email to multiple recipients, all on Bcc, so that the recipients' addresses are hidden. Or even worse, all on Cc, so that everyone sees each other's email address, as I have seen happen many times before. You need to send your email to everyone on that long distribution list – just make sure that you send separate emails and make your enquiry relevant to each person, their venue and/or their city. You will get far better results, I promise.

Common sense should prevail when you're considering ways to approach people. Think of any situation where someone is contacting you to see if you're interested in doing something with them. Someone asking you out on a date, maybe? Someone offering you a job, perhaps? Wouldn't it feel slightly less special if they copied in thirty-five other people, too? If you haven't taken the time to write a personal, individual email, don't expect anything back. Blanket emails are viewed as spam. Don't make the message about your band the spam in someone's inbox. Your band deserve better than that and so does the promoter.

I sometimes used to approach promoters pretending to be my band's agent. A third-party representative. I have no doubt that some promoters knew instantly that I was blagging it, but in many cases, it seemed to work and added credibility by giving the idea there was a 'team' around the respective band. On the other hand, the '*I'm in a band and we're absolutely great. Can we have a gig, please*?' approach may win over the hearts of some promoters. They might remember when they were in a band and needed all the help they could get.

It's worth experimenting with your approach a little but my recommendation is to explain that you're booking shows for the band, without saying whether you're their agent or that you're a member of the band. You don't need to go into that yet but if a promoter asks you directly about your role, you should be honest with them. You want to build a relationship with the promoter and they need to trust you. Try to refrain from going on about how good the band are. If you were an established agent in the industry then your opinion would carry some weight, but as an unknown entity you should be professional, direct and as factual as possible (and persuasive, of course).

Here's a basic example:

Hi Dave,

I'm booking shows for The New Band who have just released their debut single, 'New Song'. Great support on Radio Fake already with a review due out in the Fake Telegraph next week. Here's a link to the single premiere on New Music Blog yesterday – [link]

I'm very keen to get them on at 'Popular Club Night' over the next couple of months if you're interested? Ideally in early June to coincide with the next single going live.

Let me know what you think.

Thanks,
Joe

As simple as this email is, it subtly says a lot. Let's pick it apart a little:

- → The band have 'just released' a single which basically says, 'This is happening right *now*.' Promoters like to be onto something early – it's the nature of their job.
- → Great support 'already' suggests that it's early and there is more support to come. Anything could happen.
- → The link to the single just so happens to be a music blog, which emphasizes that other people are hearing and reading about your band as the email is being read.
- → 'Popular Club Night' is specific and the promoter knows immediately what you're looking for.
- → You want a slot in 'early June' to tie in with another single. This again narrows down what the promoter might offer in terms of dates and reinforces that momentum is gathering.

Write some template emails based on a similar structure that create the same sense of urgency. Keep it short and sweet, use persuasive language and don't flesh it out unnecessarily. Every time you release a new single or have some press coverage to talk about, write a template email and use that to follow up with promoters. Don't start every email from scratch, save yourself some time. Find an email that works and use it as a starting point for every email you send to the different promoters you contact and each specific show you pitch.

Don't just call everyone 'Dave', though. That doesn't go down well.

Let's look at another email approach, a follow-up to the first email. This time you are enticing the promoter to book your band because you have other shows already pencilled in or confirmed:

Hi Dave,

Further to my last email, please see below available dates in June when a show with you would fit well:

June
06 Manchester, Fake Pub
07 Liverpool, Cool Tavern
08 AVAILABLE
09 AVAILABLE
10 Leeds, Bit of a Dive Bar
11 Newcastle, Tiny but Trendy Club

What shows do you have booked already on 8 or 9 June that need a support?

The Fake Telegraph review went live yesterday, happy to share the link if you're interested.

Please let me know your thoughts.

Thanks,
Joe

This specific example is when you're looking for support slots or club night slots for your band, as opposed to headline shows. The email itself applies a little pressure while also highlighting the fact that other promoters are on board in comparable cities. Here's a chance for that promoter to be *the* person in Birmingham, for instance, who is ahead of their competitors by booking your band. If they received the first email and didn't express interest, there's a chance they may now realize your band has some traction following the second email. You also ask if they want to see the new review, rather than just sending it. This way you can at least work out if there is some interest based on how they respond, i.e. if they ask for the link. I mean, they could just look online for it themselves rather than asking you for it, but it's worth a try. You could try the same approach by offering to send a new song or video.

At the stage you're sending these types of emails, any promoter who might book your band is not going to do so with the mindset that they will make money from the show. They would be likely to be interested to find and promote new artists because they're known as a tastemaker promoter. They may run a club night showcasing emerging artists. Or it could be that they potentially want to get on board with your band early, to be your promoter in that city going forward and to hopefully make some money eventually when your fan base grows. Or they might just need a support act for a show, can't find one on that date and your email was well-timed, so they just offer it to you.

Let's do one more. This time, let's write an email to an in-house promoter that is an initial pitch based on your band being 'on the circuit' somewhat. Again, we're looking for a suitable support slot:

Hi Dave,

I'm booking shows for The Fake Band, who have played a few shows recently with Pretend Artist.

The next run of dates is in September and one will be in Sheffield. I wanted to see if you're interested in booking them onto a bill at Made-Up Venue. I came to see Pretend Artist there recently, which was a great show, and I think the venue would really appeal to The Fake Band's crowd.

Here's a link to the latest single – [link]

Happy to share some more music and info if you're interested.

Let me know.

Cheers,
Joe

In the first two email templates, your band has some recent press and online coverage that you can talk about. In this third example, you are playing to your other strengths and it may also be because you don't have much recent media coverage to mention. What the email tells the promoter is that your band are experienced, are associated with other good bands and have some 'pull' locally. You havc selected the promoter and the venue as your first choice for your next show in that city. You also know what kind of shows the promoter does and you use that to try and persuade the promoter that it would be a good fit for your band and audience. You've done your research.

As with the other two email templates – keep it courteous, keep it brief, keep it tidy, keep it professional.

A good tactic to get a response to an email is to say you're going to call. I've been in the position where I'm emailing a promoter for the second or third time with still no response and I've said, '*I'll call you tomorrow morning to discuss this if you're around?*' or something similar. With many people relying more and more on emails, and sometimes hiding behind them, the sheer threat of having to speak on the phone is sometimes enough to get a prompt response from certain people. Even if it's '*I absolutely hate this song, please don't call me,*' at least you know where you stand, and you can cross that one off the list.

On that note, if you don't have any luck with a promoter, don't burn your bridges. When you get a knock-back, be polite and wait until there's a new review or song premiere link to send along with a '*Just to keep you up to speed*' note. Often, promoters come around when they see your band is making progress and they will respect your persistence as long as you don't pester them.

You can use my email examples as a guide but the most effective way of selling your band is going to be by creating your own emails that are unique to your band and situation.

So, in a nutshell:

→ When sharing key information about your band, create urgency by implying that interest and momentum is building.
→ Take time to put together well-written email templates for different scenarios, promoter types and styles of approach.
→ Always play to your band's strengths at the time, e.g. press coverage, impending releases, other notable live shows, size of fan base, attention from other promoters and the more general industry.
→ Send separate and individual emails to the promoters you're contacting and never mass emails.
→ Test promoter interest by offering to provide more information/music and suggest a phone call if you're struggling to get a response.
→ Remember that promoters are often making little to no money by promoting your band in the early days.
→ Don't call everyone Dave.

Get a gig for a band and you feed them for one day. Teach a band to book gigs and you feed them for a lifetime.

I'll get my coat.

The Call

Half the battle when it comes to being effective on the phone is being willing to pick it up in the first place. A lot of people avoid the phone, so make sure you don't and you'll stand out. Like anything, it's all about practise. You're going to need to get out of your comfort zone and if that means getting more gigs for your band as a result, then why not?

You will have your own style on the phone, which you need to refine continually. You might be very direct, yet friendly. You might be too direct and rude. You might be very polite, yet persuasive. You might be too polite and apologetic. Or you might be none of the above. Your tone of voice is going to be key. A promoter needs to feel at ease when they speak to you and they need to believe what you're saying. You need to try and be likable, even if it's just an act.

We've all felt nervous before making a call, especially when the other person is not expecting it. What's the worst that could happen, though? If you're calling promoters, it's not like you're trying to sell them something unrelated to what they do. They book bands and you're calling about a band. The worst-case scenario is that they don't like the band or you. But that's fine.

It's surprising how quickly you become thick-skinned when you encounter rejection on the phone, and that will ultimately make you better at pitching and asking questions. It's a necessary evil. If you sense a lack of interest or some negativity, ask them what they'd be looking for. If they won't book your band, what would change that? Ask them. Try to understand what you or your band need to do before that promoter will make you an offer.

Whether it's a cold call or a follow-up to an email, have an idea of the outcome you want.

What kind of show are you looking for?
Are you looking for a support slot?
Do you have any shows or dates in mind?
Do you want to headline at a venue?
Do you have any venues in mind?

If it helps, write out some bullet points and questions before you start calling. What information do you want to tell them and what do you want from them? Think along the same lines as what you would write in an initial email. You could even put together a script to follow for the first few if you think it will help, just try not to make it sound too rigid. Keep it brief and make sure you finish that call with a next step – maybe something you need to do before they'll book you, like sending more information in an email or calling them at a different time.

If your call will be the first time you've spoken with the promoter, you're unlikely to come off the phone with an offer for a show straight away. But you might. Either way, treat the call as an introduction. If you've sent an email already but haven't heard back, assume they haven't given it much attention yet. Your call should help encourage them to read it again and to look more seriously at what you send in a follow-up email. Remember, though, where possible you should usually email them first rather than cold calling.

Try it out. Once you've sent a wave of introduction emails, give yourself a short period of time, a couple of days later, to call all the promoters. Maybe forty-five minutes. Prepare yourself, prepare your questions, prepare your list of promoter names and numbers and scribble next to each one the key details you need to reference, i.e. what you included in the email, information about your band, venue ideas, date preferences, other bands local to the promoter that you're associated with, etc.

Go for it.

You'll feel energized after those forty-five minutes. Maybe someone sounded interested, maybe someone told you to go away, maybe someone asked you to send an email. Whatever the result, you're going to get better when you next put aside another forty-five minutes. Your confidence and conviction will improve rapidly if you keep up the calling momentum.

I've worked at call centres – selling products completely unrelated to music – and the process is essentially very similar. The people I have worked alongside that got the best results were the people who would pick up the phone and make some calls. Those people who complained about their targets instead of calling were the ones that underachieved. You've got to be proactive and you absolutely must keep pushing. Some calls will be awful and some will be great, but if you're persistent you will reap the rewards. It has always seemed that simple to me. We've all been on calls where it's been awkward, for whatever reason, and a lot of that can be traced back to those first few seconds, especially when it's the first time we've spoken with a particular person. In the context of booking a gig, or selling anything for that matter, building rapport early in the conversation becomes very important because it puts the other person at ease and creates a good environment for your pitch to be heard.

A good tip for opening phone conversations is to allow the other person to speak early after you've introduced yourself. If they answer the phone and you start your pitch immediately, it's not going to land well. Always try to avoid asking closed questions, too, as these will almost always lead to one-word answers, with that one word often being 'No'. Examples of closed questions are:

→ Are you OK?
→ Did you receive my email?
→ Are you free to talk?
→ Do you like my band?
→ Are you interested in booking us to play?

Instead, ask open questions which make it more conversational and will allow you to get a better understanding of what the person's opinion actually is. Open questions may include:

→ How's it going?
→ What did you think of the music I sent?
→ What shows do you have in November that need a good support band?
→ When is the best time for me to get back in touch?
→ What's your availability like next weekend to come and see one of our shows?

Whoever you're speaking to is going to struggle to say 'No' to any of these questions and will most likely engage in some form of conversation, even if they end it wishing they'd never answered the phone.

The more you build relationships with promoters, the less cold the calls will feel. It's always worth developing your small-talk skills a bit, too, however painful you find it. Ask how their week has been so far or what they have planned for the weekend. Talk about football, or the weather, or *Coronation Street*. Whatever floats your boat. Loosen things up a bit before you go in for the kill, it will help you. People answer the phone less nowadays, especially when they don't recognize the number. If you call and there is no answer, leave it a day and try again. Maybe try at a different time of day. Once you've tried two or three times and there's still no joy, leave a voicemail. The trick to a voicemail is, again, keeping it brief and clear:

Hi Dave, this is Joe Ogden. I book shows for The Fake Band. I'm keen to speak to you in the next couple of days, if you're free, about a potential show. Please could you call me back when you get this on [number] and we can chat more then. Thanks Dave. Speak soon. Bye.

If you've got the promoter's number from a mutual connection, mention them:

Hi Dave, this is Joe Ogden. I book shows for The Fake Band and I got your number from [person's name]. He said I should talk to you about a potential show if you're interested, I'm booking dates for November. Could you call me back please when you get this on [number]? And I can tell you a bit more. Thanks Dave. Speak soon. Bye.

Don't go into a big pitch on a voicemail and don't call yourself Joe Ogden. That's my name. Keep it high level. All you're trying to achieve is for the promoter to stop ignoring you, to hopefully call you back or to respond to the email you will have also sent to them.

From the top, then:

- → Decide what outcome you want before calling and write out some questions and key pieces of information you want to share during the conversation.
- → Pick up the phone.

- → Ask open questions to get a better sense of how interested the promoter is and limit the amount of closed questions you ask, e.g. '*What do you think?*' instead of '*Are you interested?*'
- → Get stuck in and keep up the calling momentum until you're not fazed by picking up the phone.
- → Start watching *Coronation Street*.

The Pub

Right. This is what taught me how to sell a band, negotiate a fee and confirm a gig.

This is nuts and bolts stuff.

For me, the local pub gig was my first proper foray into playing live and becoming an agent. And by local pub I don't mean some cool, friendly, beardy, crafty, city pub that has a renovated back room with a good in-house PA system.

I mean a sticky, hostile, still beardy, small-town, farty pub that has bands playing in the corner of the room on a Friday and Saturday night.

Look in the Yellow Pages. Does that still exist?

Maybe look on the Internet then.

Depending on the kind of area you live in, and the kind of artist you are, find a suitable establishment to call. It could be either of the above types of pub or a bar or it might be a social club or a village hall or a community centre or a café.

Somewhere that puts live music on.

By calling the venue directly, you might be in with a chance of speaking with the person responsible for organizing the gigs in-house or you might be pointed in the right direction at least.

Go on.

I'll use a local pub example because that's how I learned.

The Crown. That'll do.

Maybe find out the name of the landlord/boss first and ask to speak with them. They might defer to someone who is responsible for booking the bands. Let's call her Sheila.

Sheila might only work on Wednesday mornings. Call back on Wednesday and tell her you're representing a band (your band), tell her the name and genre and that you're booking dates in for October/November. Mention that the band have been doing the circuit for a while, drop in the names of a couple of other live music venues but tell her the band still haven't played the Crown, therefore you'd be keen to include it on the next run of gigs. Don't ask if she's interested – just ask which Saturdays they have free. If she asks how much you charge, ask her what their budget is (remember it'll be a flat fee for a pub gig unless there's a door charge, in which case you'll need to treat it as a ticketed show and negotiate a percentage of profit from door/ticket sales). If she asks what songs the band play, tell her all the classics and mention they play a couple of their own. Plant the seed that they don't just play covers (unless they do just play covers). Tell her the recent shows have been absolutely packed and you've had to add more encores into the set.

Just roll with it.

A key thing to mention here is that I am by no means encouraging you to lie. If you say one thing (e.g. they're great live) then turn up on the night and you completely mis-sold the band (e.g. they're terrible live), word will soon spread that you're a blagger. You can exaggerate, though. Of course. Why not? Make your band and your recent gigs sound exciting. Sell your band. That's the whole point.

See how you get on and once you've booked a gig, write out ten more places and call them. Once you've got through that list, you'll be flying. I did the very same thing. I used to book pub gigs on my lunch break when I worked at the video store Blockbuster and when I wasn't watching

Titanic. When I had booked enough shows for my own band, I started booking for other bands, and the landlords/ bookers started to know who I was.

Contrary to what I've said previously, when it comes to booking local pub gigs, the fact that you've been around the block a bit will probably help you. It will reassure the pub that you're going to bring a crowd. The number of YouTube views for your recent video might not quite cut the mustard on this kind of pitch. Also, describing how good the band are (especially live) is going to help when booking this kind of show. In most cases, pubs need to know they're booking a solid band playing a solid set list who will bring a solid crowd along to watch them, and that it's something that will not upset the regulars *too* much. It's damage limitation.

As with playing the show itself, pitching your band to any promoter is all about knowing your audience. Although the pub circuit is dwindling, it still exists and is a fantastic resource for bands to get experience of performing live. The pubs need the business, too, so make sure you invite all your beer-guzzling, pork scratchings-eating mates along and keep the dream alive.

These types of shows are learning curves. Let's call them character building. I once played a metal gig at a pub and there was a round of bingo between our sets. That didn't go down very well with the lads. The last song of our first set was 'Fucking Hostile' by Pantera, too, so we didn't exactly set the stage for the bingo caller. It wasn't one of my better bookings.

If the band have to learn a few covers (maybe not Pantera) in addition to your own material, it might be worth playing some pub gigs to road-test your original songs whilst also getting paid reasonably well, winning some new fans and developing some stagecraft. Watch that scene from *The Blues Brothers* where they're playing behind a cage and they must try and win the crowd over while bottles are flying at them. It shouldn't be *that* bad. Hopefully. Maybe that will depend on your set list. I've played gigs before where we've been 'paid off' because they'd prefer us to stop playing rather than do any more.

Who's laughing now though?

Still them, probably.

Things to remember:

→ Pick a pub, any pub. Or a café, bar, community centre, etc. Somewhere that puts live music on.
→ Find a number, contact the booker and talk about how good your band are and how big your following is until you get a gig.
→ Pick ten more and call those, too.
→ Make sure you're as good as you said you were and learn some appropriate covers.
→ Use pub shows to hone your craft, to earn some money and to win new fans.

The Deal

Never pay to play. It's a scam. Dodgy promoters sometimes make these offers which mean that the artist must either sell a certain amount of tickets directly to their fans or pay the equivalent value in cash to cover shortfall. You need to decline those types of offers. It's a way for promoters to transfer their own risk to the acts performing at the venue, a risk that it is the promoter's job to bear. You've done your side of the deal by existing as a band, having instruments, being good, building a fan base, promoting the show, turning up with your gear and playing. You're the band and they're the promoter. Different jobs with different responsibilities. You should always get paid for performing.

Any decent promoter will have a budget for all acts on the bill. At small club level it's usually a nominal £50 for a support but can be much more (or less) depending on the size of the show. It might be offered as 'expenses' but, however it comes, it's payment in some form. Don't devalue yourself as a band that will play for free or worse. Again, there are always exceptions – think of Freda and her sausage rolls – but generally speaking, make sure there's a fee.

When you're playing as a support act or on a club night bill, at a pub or at any kind of free-entry show, you'll almost always be paid a 'flat fee', which means there won't be any 'overage', i.e. additional money. If you agree on a £50 flat fee to play a show then you will be walking away with £50. Simple as that.

A 'guaranteed fee' will often just be called the 'guarantee' when you're booking shows. That means exactly what you would think it means – it represents the guaranteed amount of money your band will be getting paid for playing the show. This term is used with a 'percentage deal'. These types of deals ensure a fair split of profit between the artist and promoter, the two most common being:

Plus percentage

This kind of deal means the artist earns their agreed guaranteed fee plus a percentage of profit from ticket sales. Profit is defined as net revenue from ticket sales (in advance and on the door) less agreed show costs.

The standard proportion of profit for the band on this kind of deal is 80 per cent, with 20 per cent for the promoter. However, I've seen deals where the band's percentage is anywhere between 70 and 90 per cent.

With these 'plus percentage' deals, the promoter will build in 'promoter profit' or 'promoter fee' into the show costs in the same way the artist's guaranteed fee will be built into show costs. The way a plus deal can be summarized in writing when confirming the deal could be '£250 plus 80 per cent of profit after agreed costs'.

'Plus' example:

→ Total net costs for the show equal £1,000, with the guaranteed £250 fee for the band and £100 promoter fee built into that cost figure.

→ Total net revenue from ticket sales equals £1,500, meaning it has 'broken percentage' and the show profit is £500 (£1,500 less £1,000 show costs).

→ The band walk away with their guaranteed fee *plus* their agreed percentage of profit, i.e. 80 per cent of £500 profit: £400.

- Thus, on a '£250 *plus* 80 per cent of profit' deal for this show, the band walks away with £650.
- The promoter fully reimburses themselves for the £1,000 show costs from the net ticket revenue. The show costs reimbursement includes the 'promoter fee' of £100 and the promoter also gets their 20 per cent of show profit on top (20 per cent of £500 equals £100), meaning the promoter receives a total of £200.

Versus percentage

This kind of deal means the artist earns their agreed guaranteed fee *or* a percentage of profit from ticket sales, *whichever is greater*. Profit is defined as net revenue from ticket sales (in advance and on the door), less agreed show costs. The standard proportion of profit for the band on this kind of deal is again 80 per cent.

The 'promoter fee' will not be built into the show costs and neither will the artist's guaranteed fee. The way a versus deal can be summarized in writing when confirming the deal is something like '£250 vs 80 per cent of profit after agreed costs'.

Let's assume it's for the same show as in the 'plus' deal example above. This time, though, the band's guaranteed fee (£250) will not be built into the costings as a fixed item and neither will that promoter's fee (£100). Therefore, for the 'versus' example:

- Total net costs for the show equal £650 (not £1,000).
- Total net revenue from ticket sales equals £1,500, meaning it has 'broken percentage' and the show profit is £850 (£1,500 less £650 show costs).
- The band would walk away with either their guaranteed fee of £250 *or* 80 per cent of the show profit, whichever was greater.

- → Eighty per cent of the £850 show profit equals £680, therefore, that is what the band walk away with, *instead* of the £250 guaranteed fee.
- → The promoter would fully reimburse themselves for the £650 show costs from the net ticket revenue and would also get their 20 per cent of the show profit (£850), which equals £170.

With either kind of percentage deal, if the show does not 'break percentage', or sell any tickets whatsoever for that matter, the promoter will still pay the band the agreed guaranteed fee. The aim is always for the shows to break percentage, of course, but percentage deals which include a guaranteed fee provide some safeguard for the artist.

When you need to create a budget for a show or a tour, you're going to take your guaranteed fee(s) as the absolute minimum level of income from the show(s). When shows break percentage and the artist receives 'overage', i.e. more money than was guaranteed, and if they budgeted well, it will mean the show or tour has more than paid for itself.

Show costings

This will be a cost breakdown for organizing and promoting the show and will include some or all of the following:

1. Venue rental
2. PA and lights
3. Promotion/marketing
4. Catering
5. Support acts
6. Event staff
7. Backline
8. Accommodation
9. Flights
10. Local transport

Numbers one to six will be typical costs covered by the promoter as standard and some may be broken down further. Promotion/marketing may include posters, online ads, print ads, etc.

Numbers seven to ten come into play mostly when you're playing abroad and/or a one-off show and therefore you're not on the road with your gear. All show costings will vary, so always look through them when you get the offer and, if something doesn't look right, question it. Any promoter who is above board is going to be happy enough to explain what they have included as part of the show costs and will be able to justify why those inclusions are there.

We need to talk about the rider. The catering rider, that is. You know, the list of food and drink items a band requests that the promoter provides in the dressing room ahead of their arrival at the venue. It might also be negotiated as part of the rider that a 'buy-out' is included instead of – or as well as – a standard list of items. Thc buy-out is an agreed amount of money that the promoter will give to each member of the band and crew to spend on a meal.

At small club level you're going to be lucky if there's more than £50–£100 budgeted for your catering rider. See what the promoter includes in the show costings first. Remember, lower show costs are a good thing if you're on a percentage deal as that means the break point of the show is lower. Get into that profit at the earliest opportunity, right? Don't send some silly long list with all sorts of craft beers and artisan pies. What do you need? Food? Beer? OK. As long as it's reasonable. Maybe push it *a bit*. Just don't be a dick. Of course, budgets grow as your profile does and the ticket price and venue capacities increase. Gauge your rider requests on these factors.

The settlement is something you'll go through with a promoter after the show when the deal for the show is plus or versus percentage. The promoter will provide the settlement, which will detail final show costs, ticket sales and a total net revenue figure. This is when you can compare the final show costs with the original costings that accompanied the offer and work out exactly what the band should be paid as per the agreed deal.

If anything looks odd or unrealistic on that settlement, you need to raise the question with the promoter ASAP. The final costs shouldn't be higher than agreed when you confirmed the show. If they are, then there needs to be an explanation. Most of the time these final figures will be pretty much fine, but anything extra raises the break point of the show. If that's the case, then your percentage of profit will be worth a smaller amount, so make sure you check thoroughly.

As and when you get a tour manager on board, they will take care of the settlement. An agent, manager and/or tour accountant might also be involved in checking the final settlement to make sure the artist is getting all the money that is due to them.

But until that point, it's on you.

In short:

→ Avoid pay-to-play shows at all costs and make sure there is always a fee in some form for the shows you play.
→ Guaranteed fees are termed as such when the deal is a percentage deal.
→ A plus percentage deal means the artist earns their agreed guaranteed fee plus a percentage of profit from ticket sales after all show costs are covered (including the guaranteed fee).
→ A versus percentage deal means the artist earns their agreed guaranteed fee or a percentage of profit from

ticket sales – whichever is greater after all show costs are covered (not including the guaranteed fee).

→ Familiarize yourself with the standard items within a typical show costing to know what looks legitimate and what doesn't.

→ Keep your rider requests reasonable.

→ Go through settlements thoroughly following shows.

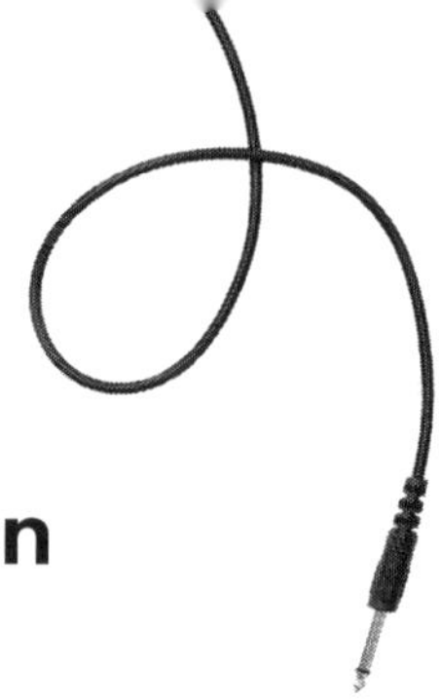

The Negotiation

Some people find it incredibly difficult to negotiate, especially on behalf of themselves. We often have a tendency to downplay our own talent and worth, and we can find the whole process of putting a price on ourselves or our band a little embarrassing.

But why shouldn't you absolutely believe in your band and strive to get good deals? If you can put all the awkwardness and self-consciousness to one side and become comfortable or even good at talking about money, then you're going to negotiate better deals.

There are many approaches you can take when it comes to negotiating and I advise you to do your own research to find styles and techniques you're comfortable with. Some will work better for you than others.

Let's look at some common scenarios when booking shows.

Ticketed headline show

Your band's worth will always increase as your profile does but you only have so much influence over what a promoter will pay for a ticketed headline show. The budget for a headline show comes down to venue capacity and ticket price, e.g. if the venue capacity is 500 and the ticket price is £10, then total gross revenue on a sell-out show is going to be £5,000. VAT needs to be deducted from that along with show costs and the artist's guaranteed fee (depending on what kind of deal it is) before there is a net profit.

THE NEGOTIATION

Once you and the promoter have decided on a venue and ticket price, ask them to send over an offer, which they will calculate based on what they believe is a reasonable expectation of ticket sales. Please note that the promoter will usually err on the side of caution with regards to expected demand for tickets and this is something you might have to challenge them on. The offer should come in the form of a guaranteed fee and either plus or versus percentage.

The offer should include show costings and, if it doesn't, you can ask for them. If you have both the offer and the costings, you can tell if the guaranteed fee is too low – based on total potential net revenue – in which case it's time to negotiate that fee up. That conversation will come down to your prediction of ticket sales versus the promoter's prediction. It's all about the risk for the promoter at this stage. The maximum your band could earn from a show when all tickets sell out compared with the guaranteed fee the promoter is offering essentially represents the level of confidence the promoter has in the show. Therefore, the disparity between the guaranteed fee and the total potential earnings for your band typically becomes smaller the more confident the promoter is that the show will sell a lot of tickets, or will sell out. If you're certain the show is going to sell out and the guaranteed fee that has been offered is significantly lower than what your fee 'plus or versus the percentage of profit' would be on a sell-out show, then you're in a strong negotiating position. The reason you want to negotiate the best possible guaranteed fees for shows is because your tour budgeting should be based on your guaranteed income from the shows and not the potential overage.

Even if you aren't that confident about ticket sales, you may challenge certain items listed in the show costings. Ask the promoter if they're necessary. If they are, leave them in. If not, ask that they be removed. Maybe some costs can be reduced a bit? Remember that if show costs are lower, the potential profit and the available budget for a better guaranteed fee are increased. This comes with experience so make sure you take the time to study those show costings to start to understand what should be included. Beware that some rogue promoters try and earn more money from the show, by trying to slip in certain 'show costs' that are either inflated or are just fake. Never shy away from asking questions when something doesn't look right. For example, if something is listed that you've never seen previously in other show costings, ask what it is. If the staff costs seem high, ask for a breakdown of what they include. The same goes with marketing or venue costs. Or anything. If something appears vague, there's no harm in asking for more clarity. In most cases all should be fine, but the promoter's expenditure for that respective show will ultimately be covered by the revenue from ticket sales to see *your* band, which means it's your responsibility to check the numbers.

If you don't really know what level of demand there is for tickets then you might want to cut the promoters some slack. If the show doesn't sell well, they will lose a lot of money if their offer to you is based on an unrealistic level of sales. It's essential you get a fair deal but it's also very important that the promoter doesn't keep losing money on your band, as if they do, they'll soon stop sending offers your way, even if they think you're great.

Festival/event

If you're negotiating a deal to play at a festival or event, the offer will be a 'flat fee' and will not be based on capacity and ticket sales. In this situation, the booker has a budget, due to the event selling tickets overall and not necessarily to see your band specifically. Your band are likely to be one of a few acts on the bill, therefore it doesn't matter how many people come to see your band (it does matter for you, of course, but not economically for the promoter). In this type of negotiation, you are trying to arrive at a price that the promoter is comfortable to pay your band and that you are happy to accept.

Let's imagine that you need a minimum of £500 to cover your transportation, accommodation and time off work (plus everything else). Don't show your cards first. If a promoter asks what you need to play at the event, say it will depend on what is included in the offer and which other offers come in for that same weekend. There's nothing worse than saying 'The band need £500 minimum' and they respond, 'OK – we can offer £500.' Because that's it, then – negotiation over. They might have offered twice that amount if you'd let them go first, but you'll never know. Let the promoter offer you what they are willing to offer and go from there.

OK. Same scenario. This time, rather than asking what you need, the promoter just steams straight in there with £500. Exactly what you need to break even. But as promoters rarely offer their absolute maximum as their initial offer, you're in a good position to ask for a better fee and to make some money on the show.

How should you respond?

1. Confirm immediately.
2. Keep it vague and say '*That's not enough to cover their costs*' and see what the counter-offer is.
3. Go in stronger with, '*The fee is far below what they would normally be offered,*' highlight the level of press and radio support they've had so far this year (or what is to come), and again see if there is an improved counter-offer.
4. Mention the capacity of venues the band recently headlined on tour (the big sell-out ones), be specific about what fee you would need to make it work, e.g.

£2,000 (entirely dependent on band and profile), and see if they match that or come close.

5. Pretend to lose interest unless the promoter will increase, and bluff walking away from the deal.
6. *Actually* walk away from the deal.

I'm going to assume you answered correctly.

You could respond with any one of those suggestions or almost any combination of them. Or a completely different response for that matter. It's up to you. It's all going to depend on the band's profile, how much they want to play the show and/or how much money they need to play the show. If the offer is for a festival, for instance, and you're regularly getting £2,000 for your band to play at similar events, you'll probably be responding with a mix of 3 and 4. Maybe even 5, if you're feeling lucky.

However, if it's a new band and the offer is for a great slot on a great stage at a great festival, you might be leaning towards just confirming due to the exposure you will get, as opposed to pushing back on the offer. You *could* get a little more money, but you might not want to risk losing the offer by playing hardball. You might be willing to only cover costs or even make a loss to be seen to be playing the kind of show that is on offer. How will your band playing that show be perceived? How does it look? Is it worth it?

On the other hand, if the gig is 200 miles away and it's providing the musical entertainment at a dog show or something else weird, plus you have no idea how many people will be watching or how much damage it will do to the band's reputation, then you might want to ask for significantly more money to consider it. Saying that, you might decide that no money is enough to play the show. Again: how will your band playing that show be perceived? How does it look? Is it worth it?

You must always consider each offer on a case-by-case basis. With more experience will come better judgement about when to negotiate, when to say 'No' immediately or when to bite the promoter's hand off. Remember that as your band becomes more established and the demand to see you grows, the ticket prices you agree for shows with promoters are going to increase and with that so will the fees.

Your 'worth' as an artist is always up for debate at whatever level you're at, but keep in mind that you will rarely lose an offer by standing firm about how much you need or want to play the show. Don't let the awkwardness of a stalemate make you cave in and accept a fee that is not high enough. Remember that even if the offer is enough to cover costs, if that figure is also lower than what you're usually paid to play a similar show, you'll be setting a precedent for the promoter that your band will play for less. And promoters talk to each other. Sometimes it is better to walk away from a poor offer to protect the value of your band. Stand your ground and it will help give the impression you are worth more, though you may need to show a bit of flexibility. Most negotiations reach a point where both sides are satisfied.

You need to work hard to establish and maintain how much your band gets paid for shows and to keep edging it upwards.

Before we move on:

- → Understanding the kind of show it is will help determine how much room for manoeuvre a promoter has during a negotiation.
- → A promoter's budget for a headline show comes down to venue capacity and ticket price.
- → For an event where you're on a bill of acts, the promoter will have an overall pot of money and the offer for your band will be a 'flat fee'.

- → With any offer, ask yourselves: how will your band playing that show be perceived? How does it look? Is it worth it?
- → Experiment with and refine your negotiation tactics to improve each deal and to keep edging your band's going rate upwards.

The Paperwork

When you accept a deal, make sure your confirmation email includes the main details and ask the promoter to confirm by return that they agree. Create a standardized 'deal memo' that you use to confirm all shows. Fill in all details you have gathered from the conversation with the promoter before asking them to fill in any information that hasn't yet been provided.

Here is an example of a completed deal memo:

Artist: The Fake Band
Venue: The Imaginary Venue, Coventry
Engagement date: 24/11/2019
Deal: £400 plus 80 per cent of profit after agreed costs

Promoter address: 21 Fiction Street, Coventry
Contract signatory: Dave Who
On behalf of: Great Promotions Ltd
Contact tel: [number]
Contact email: dave.who@greatpromotions.com
Invoicing details: Great Promotions Ltd, 21 Fiction Street, Coventry

PA and lights: Promoter to provide PA, lights and engineers at no charge to the artist
Position on the bill: headline
Age restrictions: 14+

Ticket price: £8 advance/£10 door
Tickets available from: www.imaginaryvenue.com/tickets
Capacity: 300
Confirmed local support: TBC

After both parties have confirmed in writing, you can create and issue a contract summarizing the show information and state at the top that the agreement is made between the two parties, as follows:

An agreement made on [DATE].
Between: [PROMOTER NAME] for and on behalf of [PROMOTER COMPANY] (hereinafter called the Promoter) and [ARTIST NAME] for and on behalf of [ARTIST COMPANY] (hereinafter called the Artist).
The Promoter hereby engages the Artist and the Artist hereby accepts the engagement.

I wouldn't worry too much about having ultra-detailed and complex contracts. When I started my own agency, I used to put together extremely long-winded contracts for every show. It was complete overkill and promoters picked them apart or refused to sign them. Try and fit contracts onto one or two pages. At the bottom, indicate where the promoter and artist should sign. Consider safeguarding your band further by adding the following to your confirmation correspondence and contracts:

Deposit: 50 per cent of fee to be paid as deposit 30 days prior to engagement date. Invoice to be provided by the Artist.
Sponsors: Promoter to inform of any show sponsors with an outline of their involvement for approval by the Artist.
Cancellation: The Artist will be entitled to 100 per cent of show fee if promoter cancels the performance.

If you get an agent, they will take care of contracting on your behalf. But it will be exactly that – on your behalf. The agreement is between the promoter's company and the artist; the agency is a third party and are therefore not liable should something go wrong.

You will only very rarely need to rely on a contract in a legal context, but it's a necessary safeguard. It can give you leverage if a promoter starts to deviate from what has been agreed. Once, I had a few bands playing at a festival in Manchester and the joker of a promoter disappeared. No one could find him to get their money. But I had contracts and that meant I had something to threaten him with. The fees weren't worth taking him to court over, but the contracts on their own encouraged the promoter to prioritize my bands. He did eventually pay out some money, weeks later, before declaring bankruptcy.

You will also need to discuss and agree the artist's production requirements for a show. Find out exactly what the promoter will be providing before the performance is confirmed and contracted. Does the deal include PA and lights? Does it include backline (typically, a basic drum kit and amps)? Put together a technical rider/technical spec that details your band's live set-up, including how many members, which instruments you all play, what equipment you'll be travelling with, what equipment you require the promoter to provide and a stage plan. The promoter will need to see this before agreeing to covering certain aspects of production. The tech rider is also for the production staff to study in advance of the show.

The nitty-gritty detail doesn't need to be on the contract – don't include load-in times, soundcheck times, show times, parking information, etc. Clarifying these specific details is what is commonly called 'the advance'. This happens in the weeks leading up to the show, whereas contracts are usually issued months ahead. A tour manager's job includes putting together 'the advance'. However, if you're your own agent, you're probably your own TM. Therefore, create an email template including all information you need ahead of arriving at the venue on the day of the show and send it to the respective promoters three to four weeks in advance. Or, if you just request the 'advance' details, the promoter will know what you mean and should send everything you need in their own standard format. If there's anything missing or that doesn't look right, request more information.

Here is some key advance information for the fake gig in Coventry:

Load-in time: 3 p.m.
Doors open: 7.30 p.m.
Soundcheck time: 6.30 p.m.
Stage time: 10 p.m.
Set length: 60 minutes
Venue full address and postcode: The Imaginary Venue, 45 Fanciful Avenue, Coventry AB1 2CD
Advance technical contact: Mike Unreal/mike.unreal@imaginaryvenue.com
Curfew: 12.30 a.m.
Parking details: on-street/behind venue

Job's a good 'un.

- → Confirm shows in writing with a deal memo which states all key details.
- → Keep show contracts relatively simple and high level.
- → Consider requesting deposits to arrive ahead of shows as a safeguard.
- → Put together technical specifications/riders to issue to promoters.
- → Create a standard template to use for your 'advance' with promoters in the run-up to shows.

The Show

Considering the premise of this book, it would be ill-judged of me to try and talk you out of playing shows. But shows aren't always a good thing.

Shows can be terrible. There can be a whole host of factors that can affect the quality of a show, including sore throats, long drives, poor attendance, audience hostility, band member hostility, PA inadequacy, band member inadequacy, alcohol, technical problems, venue air conditioning, rude bar staff, rude door staff, under-rehearsed new material and so on. Only some of those factors are within your control but any of them could easily mean a show does your band more harm than good. Make sure you do everything you can to limit the risk. Be prepared to overcome any of those challenges to make the best impact you can on the night. Are people going to go home after the show and like your band more – or less? It's a very basic question but it's important, nonetheless.

We've all experienced shows during which things have gone wrong, whether we've been in the band or in the audience. The cringeworthy moments when the mic cuts out or the band forget where they are in a song or there's a power cut or the lead guitarist gets attacked on stage by a 'fan' within thirty seconds of the first song. (That happened to my band in Leeds and the guitarist was my brother.)

You know, the usual stuff.

During the encore of the final show on the very last tour I played with The Jakpot, Bruce the bassist's bass broke (or a cable or amp broke – something broke, anyway). It just cut out. The bass line had left the building. There was no chance we could stop the song; it would have ruined the finale of our last ever show and Bruce quickly realized that. So, he just danced it out. He took one for the team. Almost a full song, just dancing. I've never seen him enjoy a song so much. He improvised and it went down a storm. It was the highlight of the night.

The show must go on.

Let's take a step back and ask ourselves why we want to book a show in the first place. Any show. What is the reason you want to target *that* particular promoter in *that* city who promotes a lot of shows at *that* or *those* venues(s)? And why now?

There are those obvious benefits of performing live – road-testing new songs, refining your live show, making new fans. But that can't be your only reason, and that shouldn't be your pitch to the promoter, either. If you had an agent and you told them that you wanted to play some shows, they would want to understand the reason. As you are probably your own agent, you need to have that conversation with yourself (in your head). What are you trying to gain by doing some shows? I'm going to assume it includes some, or all, of the following:

- Music industry interest
- Media interest
- Hype
- Perceived success and progress
- More experience
- More fans
- More online streams
- More EP/album sales

More merchandise sales
Actual success and progress
More money

There might be many other reasons, too, which only you will know, but how do the shows help you to achieve some or all of your goals? Make sure you can answer such a question with some good reasons for booking a performance. Avoid playing shows for the sake of it.

What else is happening to coincide with the shows you want to book and how are you going to sell the shows to the promoters? And to the media? Your fans need to understand the reason for staging the shows, too. The reason will change throughout an artist's career and, of course, there are those die-hard fans who will just want to come to any show they can. But for the most part, demand for tickets and press attention is going to be heightened for a show or tour when it is part of a 'campaign' of some sort.

Now I'm not suggesting your run of shows needs to have a tour name, as that can be cheesy. But you need to think about how the shows can be positioned to attract maximum attention, and that is going to depend somewhat on how established you are. Some events and themes to tie in with performing live:

The debut EP release tour
The support tour
The key-city tour
The other cities tour
The homecoming shows
The new material preview shows
The festival warm-up shows
The festival run
The headline album release tour
The unplugged shows

The full album performance tour
The classic album tour
The hits tour
The reunion tour
The farewell tour
The back from retirement tour
The one last goodbye tour

We are all familiar with many of the above categories and we've all bought tickets for some of those kinds of shows. Greater urgency is created for ticket buyers when the run of shows is perceived as a moment in time.

Whatever the theme, remember that shows are almost always booked through either an external promoter or an in-house promoter. An option you also have is to hire the venue yourself, but that happens very rarely once you're properly established, as it's an unnecessary risk and promoters will be better at promoting shows than you are. That's what they do.

When you're getting off the ground, though, you could put on your own show. Keep to your home town or city, where you know you'll get a good attendance. Don't hire venues further afield because you think it will look good that you're playing at those places. As a rule, only play shows in areas once the demand is there and a good promoter is interested in you or putting you on as a support to another artist.

Your self-promoted home-town show can be a great way of generating some excitement and making some decent money. One of my first bands used to do that and it was a real family affair. We used my dad's PA, the singer's uncle and cousin were the door staff, and the bassist's dad transported our gear in his van. All close family, extended family, friends and their families were there. We didn't charge that much for tickets but we did charge everyone – including grandmas. We had to. If there had been a guest list, we wouldn't have sold a single ticket, as we knew everyone. We sold tickets in the local music shop, at school, at college, at family gatherings. As we only had to pay the venue hire costs and a small amount for posters and flyers, we made a profit from those early shows which we used to fund EP recordings and to subsidize the cost of playing other shows where our fees weren't large. Those early packed-out shows also created a lot of interest and led to support slots on other bigger, local shows because we had proven we had a good following.

If you book them, they will come. Hopefully.

Let's talk about the 'wrong' kind of show. It can be subjective, although some shows and slots are going to be *obviously* wrong in how they appear. The punk band headlining a seated church venue show ... the folk singer-songwriter supported by a ten-piece funk band ... the metal band billed before a game of bingo. Think of a type of show where everyone comes away worse off than they were beforehand, one way or another. The performers, the audience, the sound engineer, the venue owner and the promoter. Worse off financially or reputationally or in terms of fulfilment and general levels of happiness. Or all of the above.

The good news is you can make time to speak to the promoter, as well as look online and ask around, and that means you will have then revealed any glaring red flags before confirming the wrong kind of show. The bad news is the warning signs aren't always so pronounced and inappropriate shows aren't always so obvious. You need to have high standards for your band which means finding out the right information to form a good picture of what kind of show it will be.

What kind of artists usually play at that venue?
What kind of crowd does it normally attract?
Does the promoter have a good track record?
Are the shows they promote usually busy?
Is the proposed bill appropriate?
What's the ticket price?
What's the usual attendance for this type of show?
What's the usual attendance on that night of the week?
What's the offer?
How is the show going to help your band?

It's your call.

Be sure to:

- → Work out why you want to do the show, what you could gain and what you might lose.
- → Make sure other activity is happening to coincide with your shows.
- → Tactically position live dates and tours to feel like they're a moment in time in order to increase interest and ticket sales.
- → Do your due diligence to establish which offers to turn down.
- → Only play shows when a promoter is involved, with the exception being to possibly promote your own home-town shows in the early days when the demand is there.
- → *Maybe* put grandmas on the guest list.

The City

Your fans' perception of your band playing in the nearest big city can be of your success and progress. The reality of your band playing in the nearest big city can be intimidating and soul-destroying.

If your band is from a small town, you should adopt a city as your own. My adopted city was Manchester, but the first band I joined there contained no Mancunians at all. I was from Burnley, another member was from Penrith, one was from Barnsley and the other was from Billingham, which was very much like a list of places visited on one of the early tours I booked. They'd all gone to university in the city and stuck around after they finished. It became their place.

Cities have the most amount of opportunities for bands to grow a significant size of fan base:

Loads of people.
Loads of students.
Loads of bands.
Loads of genres.
Loads of venues.
Loads of promoters.
Loads of gigs.

You might want to consider moving to a city as a band to be available for last-minute opportunities (as the support for a touring artist, for example) and to be generally on the scene, meeting people and making connections. If you can't move to a city, try to go into town enough to become known. You might not find it so easy to make the transition if you're the kind of tight-knit, small-town band who keep themselves to themselves. In that case, you might find the whole 'playing in a city' experience to be fruitless and futile. Plus, if all your fans are out of town, you have to ship them all in on a bus for each show you play, otherwise you might find promoters being reluctant to book you because you don't have a reliable local following.

But it doesn't have to be that way.

This is not a self-help book about how to make friends, but try to watch other city bands to begin with. Show some encouragement. Maybe your band can support theirs at the next show. Get your name out there. Play a good few shows yourselves and establish some allies and fans in the city. If you can crack it, you're on the right track to cracking other cities. Promoters in cities sometimes talk to promoters in other cities, but the people they most definitely do talk to are agents, so that they can book touring artists. If you're looking for an agent or for other promoters to book your band, becoming established and hyped in your own city is a step in that direction. Also, by being on the scene and playing different shows, you will play with bands who are travelling – from Sheffield or Leeds or Bristol or Glasgow. Anywhere. Stick around and watch their sets. Speak to them afterwards. Trade contact details. Maybe you can play a show with them in their city next?

I can hear doors opening as I'm writing this.

London is different, though. It's a tougher nut to crack, partly because it's so big. Things move quickly in London and you need to keep up. When I went to university there, in 2005, Camden in north London had been the crucible for new music for quite some time. Shoreditch was coming through and, when I returned to London in 2012, Hackney had caught up to consolidate east of central London as the breeding ground for hot new artists in the capital. You'd be hard-pressed not to bump into agents, managers, promoters, label scouts, etc., across venues in east London on any given weeknight. That was where a lot of the interesting new artists were playing and the cool gigs were concentrated. Places like Dalston, Hackney Central, Haggerston, Cambridge Heath, Old Street, Bethnal Green and Shoreditch.

But these continued to change and will go on changing.

London shows are always going to be very important in terms of how you are perceived. For artists of all sizes, picking the right bills to be on or venues to headline in the city is extremely important, as it's where a lot of the music industry and media are based. Be cautious about playing in London at a weekend, though. Unlike many other cities – unless you're very well established – a weeknight is going to serve you better and will maximize the attendance. Weekend shows can be unpredictable. You're up against an increased number of events and mainstream gigs, so competition is high. Plus, the music industry and media generally aren't working, so will be less likely to see shows. Monday to Thursday, that's the trick in London, when you're establishing your band.

Now, I'm not saying industry scouts are going to turn up to your show and sign your band just because you're playing in London. As you may have experienced already, that isn't really what happens. But if you're trying to get London industry people to come and see you play, make it as easy as you can for them. If you have some serious interest from an agent or promoter, ask one of them to help find a show for you. You might be in luck. Work out the areas where most new artists play shows, see which venues they are playing and target those same venues and promoters. Maybe it's a club night, maybe it's booked in-house, maybe it's with an external promoter. It won't be hard to find out, just look at the venue or the artist's gig listings online. Work out who the promoter is and contact them.

When you try to establish your band in London – or in any city for that matter – remember that the priority is not being the headliner or playing the big venues. Not at first. What matters the most is that your band are playing on good bills and are associated with busy shows and other good, emerging artists. What's also very important is playing for the right amount of time. Thirty minutes is optimum. Any less than that is too short and any longer is too long, in the early days. Thirty minutes is ideal for grabbing the audience's attention and leaving them wanting more. It's a snippet. It's the best of your live material.

If you're trying to get an agent and you're hoping one will come along and see you, bear in mind all the variables that can affect the way you seem to them. Some of them are outlined in the list below. Not all are within your control but do your best to avoid playing shows that might put people off. Yes, it is in an agent's interest to come and see your band if you have some momentum. They are looking for exciting new artists to represent. But don't let that one chance you might have with that agent be ruined by inviting them to a sketchy show. Or if coming to your show would mean spending two hours travelling, you might find that they're 'unavailable' that night. When I was an agent and a new artist invited me to their show, here were some factors that would have worked against them:

- Out-of-town venue
- Obscure venue
- Incoherent line-up
- Late stage time
- Delayed stage time
- No guest list

Guest list – but I'm not on it
Technical difficulties
Poor sound
Empty room
Awkward silences
Under-rehearsed songs

Don't confirm your band to play shows in any city when you have no idea if it's worthwhile, and don't waste your time and money playing the wrong shows. Err on the side of caution, always. You ideally want to try and get good local promoters interested in your band so that you have them on the ground keeping an eye out for good opportunities like supports or slots at club nights they're involved in. They may also give you some guidance on which shows not to play, as they'll probably know the scene well.

Get off to a good start in any city and the bigger and better shows will come.

Once again from the start:

- → Many more opportunities exist in cities, especially if you're based there and have built some connections.
- → City promoters tend to be in touch with agents and promoters in other cities, so getting on their radar could open doors.
- → London is more complex and you really need to understand which kinds of areas and venues would be suitable to target.
- → Avoid weekends if you're hoping to attract media and music industry people to your show, and make it easy for scouts to check you out.
- → Don't worry too much about whether you're headlining – the most important factors are the quality of the venue, the association with the promoter, the line-up and the reputation of the event.

The Venue

Venues are everything, aren't they? What would we do without them? Where would your band be? Where would this book be? Neither would 'be' at all, would they?

Bands wouldn't exist.

Promoters wouldn't exist.

Agents wouldn't exist.

The live music scene wouldn't exist.

Books about the live music scene wouldn't exist.

It's like trying to imagine the solar system before the Big Bang. You can't, really. Am I being too dramatic? I mean, they're not all great, are they? Venues. They stink, some of them. In fact, a lot of them do. What would a venue be if it didn't smell weird, though? Nice? Who wants that? In the musk we trust. There was a period in my life when it felt like I spent more time in venues than I did in my own flat. Playing in bands, watching bands, selling merchandise for bands, scouting for bands, getting sick of bands.

I started to smell like venues.

All smelly stuff aside, though. Venues are essential. They can be legendary and iconic. But they're not all right for your band. When booking headline shows, you're in a decent position because it's up to you where you play, within reason. That does depend on there being an interested promoter, adequate demand to see your band and venue availability. Remember, after those early home-town shows, don't go hiring the venue yourself if a promoter won't promote the show. The promoter is key, whether in-house or external.

You must decide what capacity level is right, look at the options at that size, come up with a shortlist and research who else has played at those same venues recently. Work with a promoter at your preferred venue. Good promoters should have a good sense of what is right for your band, in terms of the kind of venue and the capacity. An agent's role would be to make the final call, though, so although you might trust the promoter's judgement, remember that you have a say and, if it doesn't feel right, don't do it.

Venues come in all shapes and sizes, so it shouldn't matter how many fans your band have, in theory. If you think twenty-five to fifty people would buy tickets to see a show, you can still make it feel busy. It's all about the venue. Once you've found a suitably sized venue that is available on the date you want, ask the promoter to see if they have drapes or curtains in-house to adapt the space to the attendance on the night. Or perhaps they can scatter tables and chairs around to make the room feel fuller. Proactively find a solution to a lower-than-hoped-for attendance. Make the show feel busy. Make people believe they were at an exciting show. One to remember. They were there. Make them want to come to the next show.

Venues play a major role in establishing an artist at any level. They're a statement. Regardless of how many fans an artist has, the right venue can help sell tickets. The wrong venue can do the opposite. Certain venues have such prestige that they help make a show more impressive for the media. Long-standing venues of all sizes have developed their own reputation and status, from the grassroots scene right up to stadium level. And most cities have some. But they're not all right for your band. An upstairs room at a pub might be better than a seated theatre. An arts centre might be more appropriate than a rock club. A converted warehouse might be more exciting than an auditorium. It depends on the artist and their profile, and it depends on the kind of fans they have and how many.

Venues provide your early stages and your later stages. They provide stages at every level. A good promoter will help you make the right call but, ultimately, you're the one who decides on the venue as long as you're your band's agent. A good agent understands how well suited the venue will be to the show on the night, but also how it will look on a list of live dates. Does the venue suit the style of artist and the live show, and will it help to sell tickets for the show?

→ However iconic a venue might be, make sure you work out if a show there is the right thing to do for your band. Is it a suitable fit?
→ Capacity is key – you don't have to draw a big crowd to have a busy show.
→ Speak to the promoter ahead of the night to see how flexible the venue staff are with the layout of furniture and use of drapes to create an intimate atmosphere.
→ Which venues are popular and would enhance your show's appeal to the right crowd?
→ How will a show at that venue be perceived?

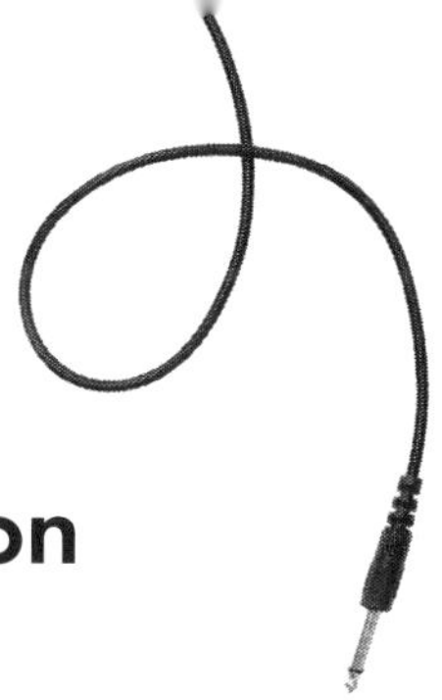

The Perception

Some shows support a release.
Some shows are for the money.
Some shows bridge a gap.
Some shows gain exposure to new people.
Some shows are under the radar.
Some shows escape reality.
Some shows are hard to categorize.

The constant across every type of show is perception; how are those appearances perceived by fans, promoters, the wider music industry, the media, by other bands or by anyone in the world that sees the shows listed. The music industry always takes notice of how many tickets an artist is worth (especially in London) and that is often measured in venue capacity for their headline shows. The choice of venue says something. It's a very important statement and size matters. Not just in London, though. Once a band is established enough to play ticketed headline shows, venue size in all markets contributes to the perception of the artist's rise or fall. The shows don't necessarily have to be huge – in fact, they could be tiny. But if the venues for the band's upcoming shows are bigger or more prestigious than the last shows they played, it will look like a step upwards, like demand is growing and, therefore, that the artist is more relevant than ever. If the upcoming shows are the same size or smaller than on the last tour, then unless it's clearly marketed as a run of underplay shows it can look like a step down for the artist. An underplay is a show that is *obviously* smaller than that which the artist would normally be 'worth' with regards to ticket sales.

Agents and promoters especially develop a knack over time of looking at an artist's live dates and making a judgement about the profile and success of the artist, as well as the potential success of the tour. In addition to venue size, their calculation could also be based on the artwork used to promote the shows, the type of venues they're playing, the amount of shows on sale, the amount of sold-out shows, the amount of non-sold-out shows, the ticket prices and the support bills.

The perception of your shows matters just as much when you're getting your band off the ground, before you're playing headline shows. What will people think when they look at your list of upcoming live dates? Is it the right show to play or does it look odd? Should they be supporting that other particular band or should it be the other way around? Shouldn't they be higher up the bill on that festival? Isn't that venue more suited to metal bands?

By playing this show, that tour, the other support slot or at another festival, on that bill, in that billing position, does it look like the artist is gaining ground or does it look like regression? For the music industry and the media, this is obvious a mile off. For fans, it can be clear, too, or it might be a subconscious perception that the artist's moment has passed.

For that reason, you're going to have to say 'No' to some offers. You might have to say 'No' to a lot of offers. You don't have to play every show that is offered to you and sometimes saying 'No' can really help your band. Quality over quantity and all that. It can increase your value. Furthermore, if the perception of your band is that you play any old show, then there's nothing special about you. You're too available.

If you only play the cool and busy shows, however, then you're going to generate some hype. If you can create some hype, then you're going to receive even more offers from all sorts of different promoters. If a switched-on promoter hears that your band are hot, they will look for you, they will find you and they will *try* and book you. Some you will have heard of and some you won't. So, do your due diligence always and check that the promoter has worked at your level or above before. Don't let your show be the first show of that size or of any size that a promoter has worked on. Don't be the guinea pig.

At whatever level an artist is, one way of generating some attention is the underplay show. An example would be a band who could easily sell out a 1,000-capacity venue in a particular city but has purposely opted to play a much smaller show, like a 250-capacity venue. A bigger example might be a 15,000-capacity stadium-filling artist choosing to play two or three 5,000-capacity nights instead. A smaller example might be an artist who could sell 500 tickets choosing a tiny, 100-capacity club show instead. It's all relative.

The underplay show may not be obvious when that artist worth 1,000 tickets plays a 500–800-capacity venue instead. That can look like there isn't as much demand to see the artist live anymore, so you need to be careful that underplay shows will be clearly perceived as such. But when done well, underplays can be really effective. By limiting supply to increase demand, you'll create excitement.
An example scenario would be to hold two nights at the chosen underplay venue, announce and go on sale with the first night in order to sell it out quickly before announcing the second show 'due to popular demand'. Make it clear when marketing an underplay show that it's not a regular headline show. It could be marketed in various ways – examples include a 'thank you to the core fans' show or a 'new material' preview or a 'warm-up' gig.

Established bands beginning a new campaign for an album release, for instance, might sometimes choose to play smaller-than-normal venues to kick off the tour. As another example, following a headline run of sell-out shows around the release itself and a run of key festival dates, there might be another headline tour that goes on sale playing the bigger venue options in the same market. Again, the way this can be perceived is that the campaign is going incredibly well and demand to see the band is soaring, hence the bigger venues on the second tour. These same principles apply in all international markets, too. Incremental steps upwards and forwards result in the perception that the artist is growing around the world.

But not all shows are fully within your control, as in you are not always the headline artist in a position to choose the venue. Therefore, when it comes to festivals and supports, you still need to make the right moves by agreeing to play shows that further your cause and that 'look right'. A good agent plays a key role in determining what the perception of a show might be and if and how the artist benefits from it. So, for now, that's up to you.

Is it the right kind of venue or event?
Which other artists have played the same show?
Is it a good association?
How does it help you progress?
What do you gain from doing the show?
What's the potential damage to your reputation?

You know what really helps ensure a positive perception of the shows your band play? If they are **SOLD OUT**. Just seeing sold out there, in bold and capitals, makes me feel annoyed with myself for not buying a ticket in time. For your headline shows, if the shows are sold out, then no one truly knows what level of demand there is to see your band. Not even the agent. Or the promoter. People can guess, based on how quickly a show sells out. But it is a guess. If the capacity in a particular venue is 500 then the number of fans the band has in that city is 500, at an absolute minimum. But it could be 1,000. No one really knows. If the shows don't sell out then, whatever the guess for attendance, the amount of people who like your band in that city is no more than the capacity. If the capacity is 500 then your fan base in that city is somewhere between 0–499. The difference is huge.

When you're considering venue options for your headline shows, then as a rule try to pick venues that have a good chance of feeling busy. Venue popularity is a factor, but most importantly how many fans do you have in the area?

As an example, if you estimate the band have 150 fans in a city, speak to the local promoter and work out which 100-capacity venue options there are. Don't be tempted to play the 300-capacity venue just because other bands you like have played there or because you think it will make you look good. It's more important that it sells out. Think about the people who will be at the show. What is their perception going to be if they're at a 100-capacity, packed, sweaty, smelly show? It's going to feel exciting and they're going to tell their friends to come along to the next one. What's their perception going to be if you're playing at a 300-capacity, half-empty, non-sweaty, quite pleasant show? It's going to seem like general interest in your band is decreasing. And that can be damaging as it could put them off and their friends, too.

Please note, an exciting show does not necessarily have to be sweaty or smelly. It could be a seated show with ample room between chairs. It could be in a church. It could be in a library. It could smell really nice.

Just as long as it's **SOLD OUT**.

Exclusivity around headline shows is extremely important, too, and will help you get your shows sold out. As your own agent, create heightened interest and demand to see your band by making sure you don't have more than one show in a particular area and on sale at a particular time. Don't spread your audience thinly across multiple venues and dates. Give them one option at a time. Direct fans to each show and keep the venues busy. The promoters would expect nothing less. There might be exceptions – for example, when you're established and extremely confident in your worth you might choose to have multiple, consecutive-night shows on sale together. That would be a tactic adopted by the agent to create the perception that the artist's profile is very strong – to the extent that one show simply isn't enough to satisfy the demand. Generally, though, keep it simple for the fans by only announcing a new show once the first show has either happened or has sold out in advance.

Simply does it:

- → Be conscious of whether each show you play appears to be a step upwards, or a step down.
- → Agents and promoters who are considering working with your band will take note of the venues you've played recently and the shows you have coming up.
- → Turn down gigs that might risk giving the impression that demand to see your band is regressing.
- → Create the right kind of perception and expect incoming enquiries from promoters to increase.
- → Underplay shows can be an effective way to generate some hype, as long as they're well executed.
- → Exclusivity around key dates is important and remember to keep your shows sold out whenever and however you can.

The Support

Support tours and playing one-off supports can be a great way to associate your band with a more successful band, if it's a suitable fit. This level of exposure can be game-changing, and not just to the people in attendance at the shows. Because of the wider impact the association has, i.e. how you're perceived by the music industry, the media and fans in the way that you are listed and promoted as the support act on a show. For example, a radio plugger's efforts in trying to get a radio station to play a band's new single can be helped significantly by the band's association with a more established artist which has strong support from the same radio station.

Try and support the kinds of artists that are further along a similar path your band would like to go down. To give your band a chance of getting good support slots, you need to be connected with other artists. The headliner's agent is usually responsible for the sign-off regarding the suggested support acts on a show or tour, but they often run suggestions past the manager, who in turn asks the artist for their preference. Therefore, if you're on the headline band's radar and your band are suitable musically, that's going to give you a better chance. That's easier said than done when it comes to much bigger artists. In that case, they may not know you personally but could have heard of your band because of another artist you supported, or you may have been on the same bill at a festival, or one of your songs might have been on the radio, or a song of yours could have been reviewed on a popular blog.

Having a proper agent would be really beneficial when trying to get good supports, because agents ask other agents for support suggestions. Agents can be the first to learn that a tour or a show needs a support. If an agent books a tour for an artist they represent, they will often send an email around other agencies asking for tour support suggestions, sometimes before the shows are announced to the public. Or they might ask the promoters of the shows on the tour to suggest good local support acts.

The agent might want both a touring main support act and a local opener, so they'll ask for suggestions from other agents and from the promoters of the respective venues. Once they have compiled together all support suggestions, they'll send them across to the manager. Agents tend to trust that other agents will put forward artists that are suitable, both in terms of genre and profile. So, as an example, you're the agent for the headline band and they're a surf-rock indie outfit: when you ask for support ideas from other agents, they're unlikely to put forward metal bands, house DJs or boy bands. Equally, if the headline band are playing mostly 250-capacity venues on the tour, agents are unlikely to put forward artists that are worth that amount of tickets or more. The support suggestions will have a relatively smaller profile than the headline artist and will, therefore, be worth less tickets than the headliner.

This does not mean you cannot get good supports for your band just because you don't have an agent. There are plenty of decent gig listing websites that are easy enough to check to stay updated regarding new shows. Sign up to mailing lists and, as soon as you see something announced that is suitable, it's time to do some research. Use your noggin (and the Internet) to work out which promoters or artists you need to be in touch with.

Who are the band?
Do you know them?
Have you played with them before?
Who's promoting the show nearest to you?
Have you worked with them before?

Promoters certainly have influence regarding the support, so you need to be putting yourselves forward to support on *all* shows or tours that you think are right for you. Remember, don't use social media or an online submission form when pitching your band to promoters. Not if you can help it. Find an email address. Keep your message brief, keep it professional and you'll be taken seriously.

Hi Lisa,

Long time no speak. Hope you're well.

I'd like to put forward The Fake Band to support The Bigger Fake Band in Glasgow on 24 November, if you're taking support suggestions.

The new EP has just been released and lead single 'Great Song' was streamed more than 2,000 times in the first forty-eight hours. A Scottish Music Blog are running a feature next week, too, coinciding with the next video going live on 16 November.

Keen to know what you think and happy to share more info if you're interested.

Cheers,
Joe

What you're *not* telling the promoter is that your band don't have a manager or an agent or that the 'release' is not through a label and is just your band sharing the music online. What you're also not telling the promoter is that your band have had no print press coverage whatsoever or any radio support and that your mum accounts for nearly half of those online streams. (Cheers, Mum.)

It doesn't say any of that, thankfully. What it does tell the promoter is that exciting things are happening, that shit is kicking off for your band. Right now.

Think of that scenario again where you're meeting someone for the first time and you're telling them about yourself. You'd focus on the positive things happening in your life at that moment, I suspect. Maybe you'd tell them about the new job you've just started? Or your exciting Christmas plans? Or maybe discuss a recent holiday you went on? You wouldn't tell them that you haven't cleaned the fridge this year yet, would you? Or that your mum made your sandwiches for lunch that morning even though you're 31? (Cheers, Mum.)

When it comes to supporting other artists, avoid accepting supports that aren't the right fit for your band. Big shows are tempting but if the association with the headliner looks wrong, then it could be more damaging than anything. Think not just about the people at the shows either, think about the people that see your band listed as the support on all of the marketing, too. How does it look? Is the headline artist still relevant? Are they still popular? Are their fans the kind of crowd that would like your band? Supporting artists that have been around for many years can be tricky. Their diehard fans from twenty years ago are less likely to care about watching the support band than those in a crowd for a more current artist. The fans for the latter might be more open to new things than the fans of the band from two decades ago are.

Let's compile a list:

→ Association with the right kinds of artists can be crucial in generating interest in your band.

→ Having friends and allies in other bands will significantly increase your chances of landing good support slots.
→ Any form of media exposure will help you get on the radar of the artists, agents and promoters involved in the shows you want to support on.
→ Your inclusion on festival line-ups will help your pitch for supports.
→ Find out if any local, in-house or national promoters you're in contact with have opening support slots on suitable upcoming tours.
→ Refine your approach and put your band forward far and wide.
→ Despite how big a potential show is, always keep in mind what the perception of any association will be and how supporting on the show will benefit you.

The Festival

Aren't festivals brilliant? All the bands and the mud and the queues and the tents and the hangovers.

Brilliant.

There are so many though, aren't there?

Which ones are good?
Which ones are bad?
Which ones are mainstream?
Which ones are niche?
Which ones won't cancel?
Which ones won't go bankrupt before paying you?
Which ones are right for your band?

You tell me. You're their agent.

It's a minefield.

No, but seriously. Not all festivals are suitable for your band and you need to understand the landscape. In my experience, some emerging artists measure their own success (or their agent's success) by how many festivals they are confirmed at. But as with anything, quantity isn't always the best metric. And that goes for the money you're getting paid, too. In the early days, anyway.

Four or five strong festival plays in a summer can far outweigh ten weak ones. What affects how good and suitable a festival is for your band will be:

- → **Line-up**: how appropriate is the association with the rest of the artists playing? How relevant are the artists on the bill this year? Who played at the event last year?
- → **Capacity**: if the festival is big, what's the chances people will come and see your band? If it's a smaller, boutique festival, will the exposure be worth the financial loss you'll make on the show?
- → **Genre**: is the festival established as part of a particular scene? What kind of audience does the festival attract? Teenage pop-superfans/young, trendy, indie twenty-somethings/middle-aged, middle-class, beardy folk/aging metalheads? Other?
- → **Stage (and line-up)**: how prominent is the stage and can you find out how central or removed it is from most of the footfall for the rest of the festival? Which other artists are lined up and how good is the association for your band?
- → **Billing position (and stage time)**: which artists are scheduled to play directly before and after you on the same stage? Can you find out which artists are playing on other stages at the same time? Are any of those artists going to attract the same kind of people who might want to see your show?

I remember one festival I played in Scotland. The band were based in Manchester and the drive was long, made even longer by the fact we put the wrong fuel in the van twenty minutes after setting off. We waited to be towed, finally made it back to Chorlton and jumped in the singer's mum's car instead.

Off we went. Again.

The festival was big, and although the stage we were playing was pretty small, all the bands performing on it were going to be filmed for the BBC. We were excited. The closer we got to Scotland, the more it started to rain. By the time we arrived on site it was a swamp. But we weren't bothered, we were going to be on the telly. We loaded our gear next to the stage, did our warm-ups and we were ready.

HELLO, SCOTLAND!

There was a maximum of ten people watching us, at the peak. We'd been rehearsing for ages, too. The rain got worse, we finished our set, loaded back into the car and set off back to Manchester. Was it worth it? Not at all. But the footage was good.

You may well be thinking that, realistically, you'd take any festival slot that was offered to your band and that it's more important for you to just get out there, play some shows and maybe earn some decent money in the process. I can understand that and I don't want to put you off, if that's what you want to do. It's up to you. Sometimes being associated with reputable festivals as an emerging artist will help propel you and will form part of your pitch when approaching other promoters, e.g. something to mention to a promoter is that a good, well-known festival booked your band. It's going to depend somewhat on how long your band have been around and how long you plan to be around for.

As the band's profile grows and as you continue to represent them until a proper agent comes knocking, why not think like an agent yourself? Think not just about the benefit of playing the festival in the short term but about how it could help you establish your band for the long term and put you on the radar of the right kinds of people. Who's going to take more notice of your band if you have a good slot on a decent stage at a respected festival – a festival, or a stage, that is usually associated with exciting and emerging new artists? Your fans, potential new fans, other artists and the industry. Who might you put off if your band are playing a rubbish slot on an inappropriate line-up? As the opening act on a wildly eclectic bill that has no real relevance to your band or the audience you're trying to appeal to? Your fans, potential new fans, other artists and the industry.

The music industry – mainly agents and promoters – scan festival line-ups to check who is playing, which stage they're on and where they're positioned on the bill. If your band keep appearing in the 11 a.m., stage-opening slots – the slots that clash with most punters cleaning their teeth or still being sick after the night before – then you'll eventually be written off as an artist who has failed to make decent progress. Take the 'second on the bill' slot at the minimum, wherever possible, and make sure that, if you play that same event again the following year, the slot you accept is either further up the bill or on a bigger stage. It's all about the progress.

Let's not forget about the money. Money is important. Money can be essential. Money might be the main reason your band want to play at a festival. Just don't let it cloud your judgement. Playing the right show is going to benefit your band more in the long run than the money will. Probably. Unless it's loads. But you know what I mean.

Think about the positioning of your band. Think about maintaining the perception that your band are on an upwards trajectory. You're taking steps forward. Making progress. Going from strength to strength.

As your profile grows, so will the fees.

Yeah, yeah. But how do we get festivals to book us, Joe?

Thanks for asking.

Your band needs to be established to a degree before a festival will offer you a slot. The main festivals, anyway. You're going to be lucky to be offered a slot if you don't have many shows under your belt. Your recent live activity, as well as recent releases and media coverage, are going to form your pitch to a festival booker. As will details about what is scheduled to happen in the run-up to the festival. Your band's recent headline tour, and its success, will act as valuable currency when negotiating a fee and agreeing on the billing (position on the line-up) with a promoter. And you know what's going to help that conversation hugely? If your recent shows were **SOLD OUT**.

Your band's worth naturally increases if tickets for recent shows sold out as, of course, it means your shows were packed with enthusiastic fans and it means some people couldn't get in. All the more reason for a festival to book your band, then.

Hi Steve,

I book shows for The Fake Band. Following the debut EP release and packed-out run of UK dates in November, I'd like to put them forward for The Great Summer Festival. Here's the premiere of single 'Interesting Song Name' from October – [Good Music Blog Link]

The London show at Nice Small Venue sold out two weeks in advance and the next London play is in May at Bigger Small Venue. Here's one of the reviews from the Nice Small Venue show – [Good Review by Known Publication]

Please let me know what you think.

Thanks,
Joe

Most mainstream festival line-ups will primarily consist of established artists. But that doesn't mean emerging bands don't have an opportunity to play. Up-and-coming talent is usually an important part of their appeal and identity as an event. Headliners attract the headlines, but the emerging artists help keep the event interesting and relevant. How does a festival booker know which new artists to book, though? As with any promoter, they need to hear about you, and they need to see that other people are hearing about you, too.

Which blogs have been supportive of your band?
Which radio stations have played the single?
Which magazines have mentioned you?
Which new music champions have tipped your band?
Which other artists have your band supported?
Which music streaming services have playlisted your music?

When you communicate to a promoter what levels of exposure your band have been getting, always try to give the impression that what you're telling them is the tip of the iceberg. Make it seem like there's plenty more where that came from, and you're simply giving them the highlights. The same goes with any promoter, not just festival bookers.

New music festivals and conferences focus specifically on emerging artists. There may be a handful of well-known headliners on the bill but most of the festival's line-up will consist of newcomers. These types of tastemaker events are a great form of exposure for new bands on the scene and if it's a good event then you're going to be on a line-up which can be thought of essentially as a shortlist of exciting new artists that have a chance of going somewhere. Many live music fans and people in the music industry (especially agents and promoters) will be on the prowl. These events are popular for providing the music industry with an escape out of the office. They are great shows to do at the right time but make sure you're ready to impress, as you'll rarely get booked to play at the same new music festival more than once. Make it count.

When an artist has some profile and festival bookers start to take serious interest, the conversation about where on the bill they should be positioned often comes down to what level the band are at, in terms of venue and capacity – particularly in London. It is common for an artist to receive an offer which bills them below someone who is arguably smaller in profile. If that happens to you, you might respond with something like:

Hi Steve,

Thanks for this offer.

However, please can we discuss the billing? The Fake Band's next London show is at the Bigger Small Venue, whereas The Other Fake Band are playing at The Nice Small Venue around the same time. Can we switch their places around?

Other than that, the offer looks good and the band are keen to confirm if we can agree on the billing.

I'll wait to hear back from you.

Thanks,
Joe

Challenge the billing position if you genuinely feel the artists positioned above your band are not worth as much as you. Look and see where their recent shows have been or what shows in which venues they have coming up. Festival promoters should have a good understanding of where artists should sit on the bill, but they're only human and sometimes might not realize exactly how one artist's profile measures against another's. You're right to point it out to the promoter when the situation presents itself and it's important your band have an appropriate position on the bill that reflects the level you're at. Just don't be a dick about it unless you really have to be.

Exclusivity can sometimes be a condition of the offer. This is common in festival bookings, especially when you occupy a prominent position on the bill. They're running a business and are trying to protect themselves which, within reason, is understandable. If a main artist on the festival bill were to be playing a headline show nearby and at around the same time, then it would make their performance at the event feel less special. Some fans may just go to the headline show instead of buying a festival ticket. As with anything else within an offer you receive, make sure you question it if it doesn't seem fair. How long is the exclusivity period? How far-reaching is the area that it covers, i.e. how many miles radius from the show does the exclusivity cover? Have the conversation with the promoter. You might agree that it is a reasonable request, or you can negotiate. Don't sign yourself up if you are prevented from playing other shows in key areas during vital periods when you have other activity planned that requires support. An exclusivity clause within an offer would read something like: 'Exclusivity: the Artist agrees not to perform within a radius of fifty miles of the Big Pretend Festival in Cardiff within thirty days either side of the scheduled show date. Failure to comply could involve cancellation of the performance with no fee.'

Be cautious of events and festivals in their first year, especially through an unknown promoter. It might seem appealing to be part of a new event, to be one of the chosen bands on the bill. Check who else is playing. There is usually a reason if other artists haven't confirmed. That might be because the promoter is unknown to agents. It might be because they're unlucky and no one will give them a chance. *Maybe* the event will be a huge success.

Who knows? But what it will likely mean is that there is some risk involved – risk that the event will be poorly attended, or that you won't get paid, or that it will damage your reputation, or that it won't go ahead at all. Risk. And risk is what you need to steer clear of when it comes to new events, because if it's a sinking ship, you'll sink with it.

Before you sail away:

- → Good festival shows can propel your band forward, even if you only have a few confirmed.
- → Weaker festival shows can do little to help you progress, despite how many you book.
- → Learn what to look for when deciding which festivals to pitch for and which offers to accept.
- → Your pitch to a festival should mention any recent successes, like positive media coverage and sold-out shows.
- → Evidence of a growing fan base, demonstrated by increased venue capacities for upcoming headline shows, will help you significantly.
- → Share with the promoter all notable exposure your band have had recently and create the impression everyone is talking about you.
- → Be careful when agreeing your billing position and do what you can to make the festivals and slots you play look like progress.
- → Respect exclusivity but if you feel that the area or time period it covers is unfair, challenge it before confirming to play.
- → Avoid playing festivals in their first year to avert risk, unless the organizers are credible and very well established.

The Tour

When I started booking tours for bands, many of them couldn't afford to have any gaps in their schedules. The hotels, the beers, the kebabs. It all adds up, you know, especially on days off.

Most up-and-coming bands on a tight budget just want to keep playing shows and to get into the swing of touring. That changes, of course – as the fees get bigger, the tours get longer and exhaustion becomes a greater risk.

When it comes to deciding on a tour period, make sure it corresponds to other activity. This is very important. Releasing new music supported by a PR/radio campaign leading up to the shows would be a good start.

If your band don't have enough fans to warrant a headline tour yet but you want to hit the road, find suitable established events and club nights in different cities. The kind of shows that don't necessarily require you to have much of a fan base yet but, by design, attract people who want to discover new artists. That's the main appeal of the night. Sometimes they're free entry. Sometimes they're ticketed, but nothing too steep, generally.

As always, study gig listings of other similar artists and see which shows appear to be this kind of show as opposed to a headline show. As an example, there might be a very popular live music night in Brighton on a Tuesday, you might find something on a Wednesday night in

Birmingham, a Thursday night in Manchester and a Friday night in Leeds. You could book a run of shows on consecutive nights as a mini-tour. If you have promoters interested in other areas, ask if they have any support slots to offer that would fit into the same run.

Artists generally want to set up a tour to keep their live activity efficient and cohesive, and in order to budget accordingly and block out a particular time period. Sometimes new artists want to tour because it creates the impression that they are making progress. A combination of slots at established nights and supports form good introductions for your band ahead of trying to book ticketed headline shows with promoters in their respective cities, as you will have had exposure to a suitable crowd. It's a good start.

Whatever the type of tour, its timing should, as a rule, avoid July and August. It's a poor period for ticket sales as people are on holiday or have spent their money on festival tickets or just want to sit in the park and drink cider. Once you've decided on the month(s), define a tour period that includes as many 'good nights' of the week as possible. It can depend on various factors but Sundays to Tuesdays can be slower on ticket sales, simply because people prefer going out later in the week. It can depend on what kind of band it is and the fans' age group. Also, established club nights can be on those weaker nights of the week, depending on whether the town or city has a healthy student population who don't care what night of the week it is. Speak to your promoters for local knowledge. Remember that, in London, Monday to Thursday is generally your sweet spot.

As a starting point, when booking a headline tour, try beginning on a Wednesday and ending the following Saturday, as follows:

Wednesday	SHOW
Thursday	SHOW
Friday	SHOW
Saturday	SHOW
Sunday	SHOW
Monday	DAY OFF
Tuesday	SHOW
Wednesday	SHOW
Thursday	SHOW
Friday	SHOW
Saturday	SHOW

A well-balanced headline run like the above would be ideal as an initial tour of ten key cities, but it is going to depend on promoter interest and venue availability.

To coordinate a tour of any length, you need to contact the promoters you've chosen to work with in the respective areas. Your pitch at this point needs to be based around something strong, ideally a release ahead of the shows so that the press coverage will help drive advance ticket sales and 'walk-up' on the night.

Ask the promoters to make their venue suggestions and to provide available dates within your tour period. You should provide a longer tour period to start off with in this case: when you're ideally looking for ten shows, give a fifteen-to-twenty-date window and go after more shows than you're aiming to include, i.e. twelve to fifteen. See what you get back and where the best cluster of available dates sit and build up the tour from there. You might well decide to play a show in a non-major city simply because the promoter is enthusiastic, and the show is a decent payer and works as a bridge date between the shows on the dates either side. Here's an example email:

Hi Karen,

I'm booking the debut album release tour for The Fake Band in February with the first single coming out in early December. Here's a review of their last show in Preston supporting The Bigger Fake Band – [link]

The album comes out on 1 February. If you're interested, could you please let me know venue suggestions at 100–150 capacity, along with available dates between 2–22 February.

Cheers,
Joe

Remember that this is the approach for booking a run of headline shows. For club night shows, you don't ask for venue availability because the nights themselves are already established. Make sure, then, that you know which night of the week if you're targeting a club night, otherwise it looks like you haven't done your research. You might even decide to include some club night shows on the headline tour, maybe in those areas where you haven't yet played. Here's how that email might read if it were to a club night promoter:

Hi Karen,

I'm booking the debut album release tour for The Fake Band in February with the first single coming out in early December.

For the Newcastle show, I'm keen to get them on at The Cool Club Night if you're interested. The tour period is 2–22 February. Are there any available slots on either Thursday 7 or 14 February?

Their debut EP came out in June with strong support on tastemaker blogs – [link to blog with music]. Lots more support expected in the run-up to the album.

Let me know your thoughts.

Cheers,
Joe

Wait to see what you get back from the promoters for the headline shows and see if the venues suggested are a good fit. If you've received venue 'avails' you should begin to 'pencil in' dates to hold the venues while you piece together the rest of the tour. Hold two or three dates at each venue to allow for some flexibility depending on venue availability elsewhere.

This is the point at which you decide on a ticket price – which you should try to keep the same or similar across the shows – and ask for the promoter to put an offer together based on that ticket price and the venue chosen. Once you have dates pencilled in at all venues, you can decide on the best 'routing'. The routing is the order of the shows and a good one will appear logical, with manageable distances between each city. A good UK tour routing example for a band setting off from Manchester would be:

> Carlisle – Glasgow – Edinburgh – Newcastle – Leeds – Nottingham – Cambridge – London – Brighton – Southampton – Exeter – Bristol – Cardiff – Birmingham – Manchester.

When putting a tour together, you might sketch out two or three routing options, based on the dates you have held with the promoters, until you're decided on the best option. Once you're happy and all deals are negotiated, you can confirm the shows. Ideally, you'll want a day off after every three, four or five dates. A recovery day off after the London show might also be wise. Again, try to keep the days off to be on the weaker nights of the week wherever possible. A trick to getting good venue availability options is to work a good few months in advance. Naturally, if you're trying to book a tour only two months ahead, many dates are going to be booked already. If you're working four to six months in advance, you're going to have far better avails to work with.

Decide when to announce the tour and put tickets on sale. Provide all promotional assets to the promoters, e.g. new artwork and recent press releases about the activity that accompanies the tour (such as a record release). Ask promoters to put artwork together (for your approval) to use locally and to have ready, ideally, in time to announce the show online. The promoters will also need to provide you with a ticket link for each show that will go live at the time of on-sale, so you should collate all of this together ready for your own tour announcement to fans at the same time as the promoters.

You could also coordinate a national advert in a relevant publication in line with the tour announcement. National ads can be effective for promoting tours, although sometimes they can make little difference to ticket sales. There can be an amount allocated to national ads in each individual show costing – this is usually a contribution agreed between the agent and promoters during the show confirmation. For small club tours, a typical contribution from each promoter is £50. The agent then organizes one of the main promoters involved in the tour (often for the London show) to place the ad.

International touring

The introduction of your band into any new market needs to be carefully coordinated with other forms of exposure, such as press and radio.

I know I'm a bit of a broken record when it comes to activity being in sync, but if there's no strategic reason for the show, you are just taking a glorified holiday. It might also hinder your chances of getting another show when you really need it, e.g. when you do actually have a single being serviced to radio in that country to set up an album release. A proper campaign.

For these reasons, you need to be patient. If there is a very enthusiastic promoter interested and it seems like their offer is now or never, ask them why the show needs to be so soon. If they are that interested and they have experience, they will understand that your band want to wait until the right time before playing in that city. Also, if you're having those types of conversations with international promoters, use that as a reason to approach or make another approach to a manager and/or an agent. It might be an indicator to them that your band are getting traction abroad and that they should take more notice.

You're probably not going to be representing yourself by the time it comes to putting a run of international dates together. You're going to have a team and, even then, an agent would still be very careful not to take a band into a new market too early. In conjunction with promoters on the ground, they would make sure there is some demand and that any show the band plays looks right as an introduction into that country or city, e.g. an established club night with a solid crowd, a good support slot on a sold-out show or a popular new music festival that gets a lot of press coverage.

However, if you choose to ignore all of my advice and go ahead and book a run of dates abroad, then make sure you do some good research both into the types of venues other similar-level bands have played and into the promoters. If you have interest from promoters in the respective countries, try to book shows that give your band the best chance of having a successful run: play small venues, play cool club nights, create a buzz. Good promoters are essential as they know their culture, they know their city, they know the venues, they know the gig-going crowd, they know much more than you. A good agent knows which promoters are reliable and which to avoid, so you need to carefully consider who you commit to working with on any shows. Look at which other shows they have promoted and look at which other bands they have worked with. Due diligence is key to safeguarding your band and to avoid that fancy-sounding international tour being an absolute disaster.

Limit the shows to one or two per country. Don't spread your dates too thinly by trying to play multiple cities in new markets too early. Keep it exclusive in order to maximize interest and attendance. The capital city run is a good example and it's often where the media is focused, too.

If you're driving, try to keep the distances between shows at a manageable length and give yourselves plenty of time to allow for any setbacks. Use days off as travel days and make sure you're on top of your game at every show or it could be the only time you play there.

I remember one drive my band had to do from Rotterdam in the Netherlands to Kiel in Germany on the day of a show. It's about 600 km – which is too far but doable at a push. But we didn't make it. We had a blowout on the Autobahn and, by the time we had been towed and the tyre had been replaced, we couldn't make it to the venue in time. We had to cancel the show. We eventually did make it to Kiel on a later tour. In fact, the show there was the one I mentioned earlier, when the bassist did the emergency dancing. Maybe the fans there that night wished we'd broken down on the way to that show, too. (Sorry, Bruce.)

Before you begin putting a tour together, let's have a quick recap:

→ Choose a tour period that corresponds with other activity and avoid mid-summer months.
→ Consider booking a run of non-headline shows to introduce your band into new areas before trying to play headline shows.
→ For a headline tour, provide promoters with a tour period for them to gather available dates at suitable venues.
→ Hold two or three dates with the promoters in each area you intend to play and decide on the best routing (order of shows).
→ Confirm the shows and coordinate announcement and on-sale with the promoters.
→ Be very careful before committing to shows in other countries – if it's not part of a wider strategy within the territory, it's probably too soon.
→ Be very selective when it comes to the offers you accept and the cities you play.
→ Research which other artists have played the same venues and have worked with the promoter.
→ Use any interest from international promoters as a reason to contact or follow up with good agents and/ or managers.

Now it's time to start rehearsing.

The Agent

There is a mystery that surrounds the world of the agent and I think a lot of that is because people don't fully understand what they do.

When I had to try and explain to someone what I did for a living, it would go something like this:

THEM: So, what do you do, Joe?

ME: I'm a booking agent for bands.

THEM: Oh ... like a travel agent?

ME: No, I organize their gigs.

THEM: So ... you manage them?

ME: No, I coordinate their live shows. Only the live stuff.

THEM: Ah, I get it. You're a promoter!

ME: Yeah, yeah ... I'm a promoter.

So here is some clarity.

Agents are responsible exclusively for the live shows of an artist. Artists are typically represented by one agent or agency within an agreed territory.

Agents do not manage the artist.
Agents do not promote the shows.
Agents do not promote the artist to the press.
Agents do not promote the artist to radio.
Agents do not release the artist's music.
Agents do not book the artist's holidays.

Agents build a network of promoter contacts across their territories, they find suitable opportunities for putting forward the artists they represent, they persuade the promoters to book the artists, they respond to enquiries, they route tours, negotiate deals, liaise with artist managers, confirm shows, issue contracts and oversee the promotion of the shows.

And that's an overview.

An agent is a crucial member of the team and does much more than just booking the shows. Live performances are one of the most public things an artist can do, which can have a huge impact on the trajectory of their career. Agents have to develop a plan of action for each artist they represent. One of their main responsibilities is to protect the artist and their brand from doing the wrong kind of show. And there are many more of them than there are the right kind of show.

I was 24 when I started at a proper agency, after almost ten years of booking as many gigs as I could. What really surprised me at first was how often I had to say 'No':

No to the wrong kind of promoter.
No to the wrong kind of show.
No to the wrong kind of fee.
No to the artist's position on a bill.
No to the artwork proposed for a show.
No to the support bands proposed for a show.
No!

No for the right reasons.

Before then, I had measured my success as an agent in quantities:

How many bands did I represent?
How many gigs did I book for that tour?
How many gigs did I book that month?
How many bands did I have touring at the same time?
How much commission did I bring in?

But that is *not* what success is. Not *really*.

Success as an agent is finding the *right* new artists to represent and booking them the *right* shows in alignment with other activity, like releases and media coverage. A successful agent speaks to the *right* people to get their bands in the *right* venues on the *right* bills at the *right* time, to play with the *right* kinds of established artists in the *right* markets to help propel them to success.

Right!

Think of it as being a situation in which you've only got so many chances. You've only got so many 'chips', like in a game of poker. If you play too many opening slots at festivals, support too many terrible indie bands from the early Noughties and/or cancel too many headline shows that haven't sold enough tickets, then you're going to use up all your chips.

All those 'No' responses are to reserve the artist's chances – all those 'chips' they have – and you need to apply the same approach for your band for as long as you're representing yourselves. When the stars align for an artist, when they've mostly made the 'right' moves, then the agent is going to book them to play shows far and wide. The right shows, that is. The artist is going to be everywhere. A high volume of headline dates and festivals at the right time will consolidate the band's position as a breakthrough artist.

Booking the tour and the festival run can seem like the easy bit when you consider the complexity of trying to 'break' a band. Strategic planning and selective booking continue all the way through an artist's career in order to maintain their success and that of the agent over a long period. Any agent that is prioritizing the money over the maintained success for the artist is not going to stand the test of time.

An artist's main agent in Europe, who is often UK-based, is *usually* responsible for 'exclusive representation worldwide excluding North America'. This basically means they book all shows outside of the US and Canada, and sometimes South America, too. You'll need a separate agent, who is often US-based, to cover those markets. By having one or two primary agents, there can be a comprehensive and consistent approach to international touring, as opposed to having individual agents in many different countries. Good agents will work with good and trusted promoters in all international markets to find good shows.

There are sometimes exceptions, when a subagent is responsible for the live shows within a specific – and usually smaller – territory. Subagents act in the same ways as your normal agent but are usually specific to one market, such as a European country. Good subagents will carefully pitch and position the band to their local promoters to find the most suitable shows and festivals for the artist. It can be tempting to work with subagents in the beginning, especially when there is a lack of interest from the main agencies, most of which are in London. But be careful what you commit to. If your band are aiming for worldwide success, you're going to benefit from having a centralized agent to coordinate international touring. However, if you're already working with subagents, it can put the main agencies off down the line, as it is harder for them to effectively execute live strategies when other agents are involved, each with their own plans.

The standard commission for an agent is 10 per cent of each show fee, meaning an agent begins to earn more as the artist's profile grows and the show fees increase. When a band attains superstardom status, there might be a renegotiation of that commission rate, but that will depend on the circumstances and the artist-manager-agent relationship. The rewards can be plentiful for an agent if the artist achieves success. But for every artist on the roster which breaks through, there'll usually be others that don't, but who still require a good amount of attention and effort.

It's all part of the job.

The Outro

When I worked in London, I had a friend who was a doctor. A doctor who loved music. I remember chatting over a drink one night about how insignificant I thought being a booking agent seemed compared to her job. Perhaps I'd had a bad week.

What she said to me though was that going to see artists live, and listening to music in general, was very important to her and helped give her a life outside of work. Something to look forward to in the evening or at the weekends, to enjoy with friends and to take her mind off the day-to-day. That always stayed with me and although being a musician or an agent is not comparable with saving lives for a living, it still has its place and its purpose, and is hugely important for many people. For the people who need to let their hair down; for the people who need a distraction; for the people who want to sing along; for the people who want to get leathered; for the people without a reason. For the people.

The grassroots music scene is essential because of its accessibility, affordability, locality, variation and creativity. It's where the exciting stuff happens and where the mainstream gets its feed of emerging artists. No household name artist has got to where they are without playing on those early stages. The stages where magic happens. Yet live music venues across the UK continue to close, due largely to business rate increases, rising rents and residential development projects nearby.

Many towns and cities have been impacted since the mid-Noughties and many venues I once played in have since closed. Meanwhile, the mainstream booms thanks to the role those smaller venues once played when the artists were getting off the ground, when they were figuring out what works and when they were building a fan base.

Never has booking your band to play shows been more difficult, considering the relentless battering of the grass-roots scene and the dwindling number of venues for shows. But you can't let that stop you. What better time than now to improve at booking gigs? Get involved. Book some shows. Go and watch other bands and buy some drinks while you're there. Support the bands. Support the venues.

Support the future.

Performing live is what keeps many musicians focused on learning and practising. It certainly motivated me. When I was a young drummer, gigs were the holy grail. They just seemed so cool, and touring musicians seemed so accomplished.

The first live performance I remember doing was when I was 8. It was at a school event and my brother was on the keyboards. He was 10 and a far more seasoned performer, obviously. Our repertoire as a two-piece was limited to 'Love Is All Around' by Wet Wet Wet and 'Billie Jean' by Michael Jackson. Both were instrumental versions and we alternated between them until we were asked to stop. At least no one attacked either of us on stage that time, though perhaps it came close.

Musicians and artists of all types perfect their craft over many years. It's about effort, it's about attitude, it's about determination, it's about persistence and it's about practise. Much like becoming an agent, you could say.

Yet, after all that commitment and graft as a musician, the rewarding shows aren't always easy to find.

The shows that have an audience.
The shows that have a good audience.
The shows that have a big audience.
The shows that pay well.
The shows that look right.
The shows that sound right.
The shows that feel right.
The shows that are worth showing up for.

The shows that justify all those years practising and imagining you're playing at one of those types of shows.

Playing live is an opportunity to impress and to get feedback. Feedback is crucial and helps you to grow. The better your band are at playing live, the more fans you pick up and the more shows you can book. You're only going to find out what works and what doesn't if you have a stage to perform on.

What many musicians and artists want ideally is someone to book shows for them. Good shows, with good fees – and lots of them. So that they can concentrate on doing what they're good at, which is drinking beer ... I mean, playing their instruments.

I've known many people who were great musicians but whose bands struggled to get any interest from the industry and were left to their own devices. They had to play those scrappy, unpredictable, sometimes damaging shows to make some money and to justify to themselves why they were in a band or even played an instrument in the first place.

When I was an agent, I came across so many bands that were just not getting the traction or the interest they had hoped for or, indeed, believed they should be getting. Agents, understandably, must be ruthless in separating the wheat from the chaff, if you'll pardon the expression.

I'm not saying your band are the chaff – or the wheat for that matter. However, agents, managers, labels, publishers ... you name it, need to commit their time and efforts to the artists they really think have a chance of becoming successful. Most of the time, anyway.

But any artist who hasn't got representation can also find and book good shows. They shouldn't wait around for someone else to say they'll do it for them. In fact, they can represent themselves and book the right shows to further their cause and help demonstrate to the industry that they too have a chance of becoming successful. If you and your band have been slogging away for some time and you're beginning to feel like the ship has sailed, it doesn't necessarily mean your chance has passed. It just means you might need a rebrand. Check out these band names:

1. Smile
2. On a Friday
3. Sweet Children
4. Seymour
5. Warsaw
6. The New Yardbirds
7. Pen Cap Chew
8. The Polka Tulk Blues Band
9. The Young Aborigines
10. Cans of Piss

You know what they have in common? They're famous and we all know who they are. At least, under their subsequent names:

1. Queen
2. Radiohead
3. Green Day
4. Blur

5. Joy Division
6. Led Zeppelin
7. Nirvana
8. Black Sabbath
9. The Beastie Boys
10. R.E.M.

I'm not saying your band name is bad. Many artists were called something else until they got as far as they could under that guise. Maybe their original name did hinder progress, as I suspect it might have for one or two of those above. Or maybe they'd been around a while and things just weren't happening.

Make yourselves relevant. Have a refresh. Relaunch with new material and a new name. Become the hot new band. Go after all of those promoters who seemed to have gone cold. You might not want to mention what your old band achieved but rather approach them as a new outfit with all the potential of any new emerging artist.

Only you know what stage you're at, but don't think your current band or name is the only chance you've got. Buy back into the game and get yourself some more chips.

However long you've been around for as a band, having a more considered and structured approach to booking shows can result in better shows and more shows or less shows. It's up to you. Whether it's to help position your band as a viable outfit – one worthy of investment from the industry – or to become your own booking agent for ever, remember that what you get out of this process will largely be a result of your own efforts. As I said at the beginning, you're going to need to put in the work yourself.

Don't forget, though, that no artist has ever taken themselves all the way to the top without a team of people supporting them. It's about taking it as far as you can, or as far as you need to.

If you're good at DIY, unlike me, and you're trying to renovate your house, you might do a bit of painting or varnishing. A bit of wallpapering, maybe. You might even tile the bathroom if you're showing off. But would you attempt the rewiring? Or plumb in a new boiler? Would you try and build an extension? Probably not. You'd get the professionals in. The people who do it for a living. The people who know how to not make the house collapse or explode. Hopefully.

You can make a start yourself, though.

Good luck.

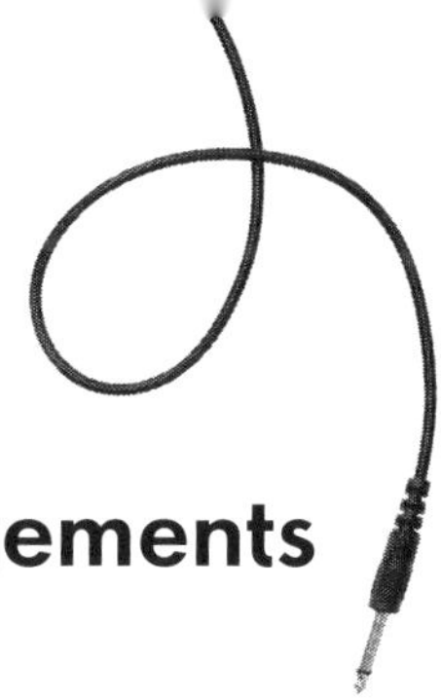

Acknowledgements

I must start by thanking my parents (and our old neighbours) for letting me play drums every day in our terraced house, for allowing me to hog the house phone to annoy pub landlords and for pushing me to follow my dreams.

I'd like to thank the one and only Charlotte Keddie, for the encouragement and patience which made it possible for me to finish this and for the (brutally) honest feedback that helped me remove most of the crap bits.

I owe much of my understanding about the live music business to Jeff Craft, the wisest agent I know. Thanks for giving me a chance. Thanks also to Jo Biddiscombe for showing me the ropes, and to everyone else at X-ray Touring.

I'd like to thank everyone in Manchester who helped me get off the ground, particularly Dave Smith, Matt Johnson, Gary McClarnan, Richard Jones, Clare Goodchild, Mark Bruce, Matt Watkins and Andrew Carthy.

Thanks to Martin Shorrock and Richard Young for teaching me how to play the drums.

Thanks to each and every artist and manager who let me work with them, with special thanks going to The Travelling Band and Meilyr Jones. A big shout out as well to all members of the bands I played in; in particular Emmott Garnett, Nathan Gibbons and my brother Martin Ogden, who all endured those early northern tours that were my fault.

I'm extremely grateful to Lucian Randall for the writing guidance and editing expertise, to Sandra Friesen for making this book look so good and to Kasia Murphy for her PR magic. Thanks for helping me get this over the line. Thanks also to all of my friends who read early drafts and provided invaluable feedback throughout the process.

And thanks to you for reading this. It means the world to me that you chose to give my book a try.

Finally, I'd like to thank my literary agent, Joe Ogden. He has no idea what he's doing but none of the other agents were interested.

Thank you and goodnight.

Printed in Great Britain
by Amazon

32847706R00075